A
NOBLE
ANGER

THE MANSLAUGHTER
OF
CORPORAL JONATHAN BAYLISS

A sequel to 'Red 5'

David Hill

Nemesis Books (2022)
ISBN: 979-8-8342-7923-5

The author is a retired aircraft engineer, spending much of his career as an avionics and aircraft project/programme manager in the Ministry of Defence. After retiring in 2004, he assisted families and Coroners in the Nimrod XV230 and Hercules XV179 cases. Also, Charles Haddon-Cave QC's Nimrod Review (2008-9) and Lord Alexander Philip's Mull of Kintyre Review (2010-11).

By the same author, in paperback and Kindle:

Their Greatest Disgrace - The campaign to clear the Chinook ZD576 pilots

ISBN 979-8-8429-8674-3 (2016)

Kindle version includes the submission to the Mull of Kintyre Review

Breaking the Military Covenant - Who speaks for the dead?

ISBN 198-1-0384-26 (2018)

Red 5 - An investigation into the death of Flight Lieutenant Sean Cunningham

ISBN 978-1-7061-4923-1 (2019, updated 2021)

The Inconvenient Truth - Chinook ZD576: Cause & Culpability

ISBN 979-8-5184-5820-8 (2021)

All titles published by Nemesis Books.

The issues related in these books are ongoing, and they will be regularly updated. If you have purchased a previous edition, please contact the publisher for a free Kindle or pdf version.

bigdee60@yahoo.com

This book is dedicated to:

Jonathan's parents Michael and the late Jennifer, and his sister Gayle and her husband Matthew.

All aircrew, and those who support them.

Rear cover image taken by Jon Bayliss during the outward flight from RAF Scampton, 20 March 2018.

All proceeds to St Richard's Hospice, Worcester

https://www.strichards.org.uk/raise-funds/

Acknowledgements

Mr Michael Bayliss & Mrs Gayle Todd

Keith Belcher

Captain Robin Cane, pilot.

Flight Lieutenant James Jones, engineer

Graham Miller, engineer

Brian Wadham, engineer

And the many aircrew and groundcrew, past and present, who approached me offering help, but wish to remain anonymous. Thank you.

Contents

Figures

Jonathan Harvey Bayliss 1977-2018

(with kind permission of Mr Michael Bayliss and Mrs Gayle Todd)

Introduction [1]

Hawk T.1A XX204, of the famed RAF Aerobatic Team the Red Arrows, piloted by 'Red 3' Flight Lieutenant David Stark and with Corporal Jon Bayliss in the rear, was one of five flown from their base at RAF Scampton in Lincolnshire on the morning of 20 March 2018. The sorties were staggered because each pilot would be spending an hour in the simulator. The route was via the Scampton-Lichfield corridor at 14,000 feet, dropping to 9,000 in the Swanwick Military Area, low level through the Machynlleth Loop in West-Central Wales, and then through the A5 pass to Anglesey and RAF Valley.

Flight Lieutenant Stark had joined the squadron the previous August. The aim was to provide him with some flying and simulator time before the summer display season began. Also, it served as a familiarisation flight for Jon and two other members of 'Circus', the team of engineers who travel with them to displays.

The intention was to then perform a PEFATO (Practice Engine Failure After Take-Off) before flying back to Scampton. Flight Lieutenant Stark had not performed one for seven months, and in his own judgment needed to because hitherto (in 100 Squadron) he performed one at least twice every month, but not at the Red Arrows heavier aircraft weight.

At 1325 hours, while attempting the manoeuvre, the aircraft crashed on the airfield at RAF Valley. Flight Lieutenant Stark ejected successfully, at 38 feet Above Ground Level and 0.52 seconds before impact, sustaining a major injury. Jon did not eject, succumbing to smoke inhalation (hydrogen cyanide, prevalent in plastics) after being knocked unconscious at impact.

*

A Service Inquiry was convened, reporting on 24 April 2019. It concluded that the cause of the accident was the aircraft stalling, with insufficient height to recover. It reiterated that lack of continuation training in manoeuvres such as a PEFATO could result in skill fade. It was likely the pilot, although experienced, was suffering from fatigue

---

1 Details of accident taken from XX204 Service Inquiry report, DAS/SI/02/18, 24 April 2019.

and distracted, which may have reduced his situational awareness. Also, he may not have fully appreciated the hazards due to an unknown aerodynamic feature of the Hawk.

Jon could not recognise the criticality of the quickly unfolding situation, and was given no warning. The aircraft design meant the pilot could not eject him. This was a root cause of death, as distinct from cause of accident. (A factor is a root cause if its removal from the problem-fault sequence would have prevented the undesirable outcome).

*

Service Inquiries look at Legal (and hence Illegal), Technical and Airmanship issues. This book takes the same approach. I am an engineer by trade so can speak to the technical matters, including the application of MoD's Safety Management System; which also encompasses legal obligations MoD staff are under. When discussing airmanship, I have drawn on the expertise of serving and retired Hawk pilots, and I am grateful for their candour. I am in no position to pass judgment on aircrew, and do not; but do note and discuss differences between the views of these pilots, the Service Inquiry report, the regulations, the known facts, and what MoD told the Coroner's Court. It is clear to me that Flight Lieutenant Stark was, in many ways, as much a victim as Jon.

As there has been no investigation by the police or Health and Safety Executive, I believe the correct approach to legal matters is to take cognisance of the guidelines issued by the Crown Prosecution Service and Chief Coroner. I do not challenge these, but discuss why they do not sit well beside MoD's regulations. My assessment is therefore restricted to the Coroner's Inquest, and compares and contrasts the decisions with those made in other military accidents; especially the previous Red Arrows fatality, that of Flight Lieutenant Sean Cunningham in 2011.

I will mention this case often. There, the regulator, the Military Aviation Authority, was directly involved in creating the risk that killed Sean; in doing so, breaching many of its own regulations. It was also the Convening Authority for the Service Inquiry, investigator and final arbiter, and so was allowed to judge its own case. Compounding this, it then participated in the prosecution of an entirely innocent party, the ejection seat manufacturer Martin-Baker. Together, that makes for an accident-enabling and unjust system, and I will explain the common factors between the accidents, and their contribution to Jon's death.

The purpose of this book is two-fold. To discuss the facts that were not revealed by the Service Inquiry or disclosed to the court, and assist the Coroner - and most importantly the family - uncover the truth. To that end, it has been written with the full cooperation of Jon's family, and the manuscript was submitted to the Coroner and Flight Lieutenant Stark's solicitors.

Figure 1: Hawk T.1A in Red Arrows configuration *(MoD)*

1. The Hawk T Mk1

The origins of the Hawker Siddeley Hawk lie in Air Staff Target 362 drawn up by the RAF in 1964, the intent being to replace the Folland Gnat T.1 and Hawker Hunter T.7 training aircraft. However, that early work moved off at a tangent, resulting in the SEPECAT Jaguar; leaving the Trainer programme unfulfilled. It was clear that, with both Gnat and Hunter now into the second half of their lives, the requirement would still need to progress, and in 1968 Hawker Siddeley commenced concept work on a design capable of combining advanced flying and weapons training. The HS 1182 programme was born.

Of around 20 candidate designs, what later became recognisable as Hawk was chosen by the company. In 1970, the RAF issued Air Staff Requirement 397, there being minor differences between this and HS 1182. Agreement was reached with MoD as to further design changes, and in 1971 the company bid the HS 1182AJ variant. This was successful, and a contract was let in 1972 for 176 aircraft. All aircraft were built using production tooling - there were no prototypes. Ground and flight tests were monitored and verified by the Royal Aircraft Establishment at Farnborough, and the Aircraft and Armament Experimental Establishment at Boscombe Down.

The aircraft was designated the Hawk T Mk1. It first flew in August 1974, and was then produced by successor companies British Aerospace and BAe Systems. The first T.1 was delivered to the RAF on 4 November 1976, fully replacing the Gnat in the jet trainer role by 1979.

Eighty-nine aircraft were later modified to T.1A between January 1983 and May 1986, and it is these that took over the Hunter role; which remained in service until the early 1990s. They were used to teach air combat, air-to-air firing, air-to-ground firing, low-flying techniques and operational procedures, and were fitted with under-wing pylons capable of carrying air-to-air missiles, high explosive rockets and unguided bombs. Also, an ADEN Cannon pod underneath the fuselage centreline. They also acted as aggressor aircraft, replicating the tactics, techniques and procedures of potential adversaries. With the exception of 19 aircraft for the Red Arrows and various HQ tasks, and 22 held in reserve, they were retired in March 2022. But, while MoD says the aircraft has been 'retired', 41 remains a significant fleet, and many of the activities required to keep them flying are not volume-related. I return to this important but oft-overlooked point later, as it played a major part in the loss of XX204, and Jon's death.

*

The Red Arrows have used Hawks since 1979, and fly a mix of T.1, T.1A and T.1W. One major difference is their aircraft have a display smoke generator system, which emits three separate coloured vapours by injecting diesel into the jet pipe efflux under air pressure. White is the natural colour of the vapour, with red and blue created by injecting dyes. The diesel and dyes are contained within a non-jettisonable 3-tank smoke pod fitted underneath the fuselage on the centreline, replacing the gun pod. A simple ON/OFF smoke management panel is added to the cockpit, with the smoke generation motorised valves controlled by re-allocated switches on the front cockpit control column handle.

I discuss later the background to the T.1W, a Mark which, as of February 2022, the Red Arrows agree they fly; but which other parts of MoD deny any knowledge of, except to say it predates the T.1A. This difference in understanding of a configuration control, and hence functional safety matter, is the first indication of systemic failings.

2. Systemic failings

MoD's position, put by Edward Pleeth QC at the Pre-Inquest Hearing in May 2021, was and remains:

> 'The death did not occur as a result of systemic failure. The act was caused by the aircraft stalling without enough height to give sufficient time to recover. There is no evidence of systemic failure'.

Each sentence in this short statement is untrue, and must be refuted because it served to divert attention from actions by senior officers and officials which carried custodial sentences. There was no challenge in court, but as I will explain the Coroner later accepted my submission that there *had* been systemic failings. She characterised this as negligence, but not *gross* negligence. I will explain why I believe she was misled into erring.

*

By definition, a systemic failure is *of a system*. The failure must affect the whole system or organisation, and be persistent. (Whereas 'systematic' refers to something that uses or follows a system or method). One must therefore define that system. Here, I scrutinise the application of MoD's Safety Management System.

It is MoD's default position that any failings are one-offs. Once the particular problem on the accident flight is identified, little thought is given to the wider consequences and there is no trend analysis or read across to other aircraft; made worse by a lack of corporate memory. All these failings occurred here.

In his 2009 Nimrod Review, Charles-Haddon-Cave QC confirmed the evidence to him that there had been critical failures, and they were systemic. He had been informed of these by members of the public, who submitted corroborating internal reports from the RAF's Director of Flight Safety. This same evidence was presented to the 2011 Mull of Kintyre Review, and accepted by Lord Alexander Philip when recommending that the gross negligence findings against the Chinook ZD576 pilots be overturned. (Mull of Kintyre 1994, 29 killed). And therein lies the first reason for MoD's claims. Recurrence, knowing the aim of Service Inquiries and Inquests is to prevent recurrence.

The primary evidence of these breaches lies in 12 common factors between the death of Flight Lieutenant Sean Cunningham in 2011, and that of Jon in 2018. I will discuss these later when dealing with the Coroner's Inquest.

*

When is a failure systemic? There are two arguments. One, that a failure to carry out a single risk assessment is a failure of the Safety Management System, and therefore a 'systemic' failure. Two, that it is necessary to show serious failures to address more than one risk, or multiple failures to address the same risk.

The first makes it easy for the prosecution, but difficult for the courts as they would not know if there were wider organisational failures, in turn making sentencing and punishment difficult and potentially disproportionate. The second is slightly more difficult to prove in that it requires historical evidence which MoD controls.

The Nimrod Review confirmed that the single but long-term failure of senior management to ensure airworthiness regulations are implemented, is systemic; as it applies across all aviation. This led to the complete breakdown of the system under consideration.

These were exacerbated by persistent directives that staff disregard legal obligations and make false declarations that the regulations *had* been implemented. This consciousness and premeditation becomes important later when considering the offences committed.

The gravity of these violations requires a high bar of proof, and to that end I will show non-compliance with each of the factors that courts must take into account in determining the degree of culpability, namely:

- Failing to put in place <u>and</u> implement measures that are recognised standards.
- Failing to make appropriate changes following prior accidents or incidents exposing risks to health and safety.
- Allowing breaches to subsist over a prolonged period.

I will set out the irrefutable evidence that MoD has catastrophically and repeatedly failed on each count over a period of decades. This is the approach I adopted in my evidence to the Nimrod and Mull of Kintyre Reviews, and to various Coroners, so I will refer to these past submissions occasionally.

I do not need to accuse. I simply quote MoD's own words from official papers and explain them. The real challenge is not proof, but that MoD is permitted to conceal evidence and judge its own case.

*

MoD will always seek to deflect and dismiss. Its mistake here was to deny something that had already been established by legal review, and admitted in its own Service Inquiry report. Even so, it almost succeeded. It was only in 2021, in evidence to the Coroner, that the truth was exposed.

However, Coroners cannot impose punishment or sanction. Nor are they permitted to voice concern over being misled or lied to in court if this only becomes apparent after the Inquest is closed. I am grateful to the Senior Coroner for North West Wales, Ms Katie Sutherland, for clarifying this (quite bizarre) point to me.[2] In that sense, MoD's strategy was successful, as it managed to conceal vital evidence until it was too late to present in court. That is for the legal establishment to deal with.

*

'A Noble Anger' is my fifth book on this general subject. I am all too aware of, and have tried to minimise, repetition. But by definition systemic failings involve repetition. Not only that, it has been the same failings each time. Legal reviews and various Coroners have confirmed this, and the government has directed that MoD corrects them. Yet it persists - in this case repeating breaches from 2011, in turn repeating failings from previous fatalities. That the government tolerates this is perhaps the worst systemic failing of all.

---

2 E-mail Sutherland/Hill, 6 June 2022 10:32.

3. Safety Management

Some important definitions

Flight Safety describes a collective endeavour to operate in the aviation domain safely, and embraces any activity that contributes to the safe operation of military airworthy systems in flight or on the ground.

Air Safety is the state of freedom from unacceptable risk of injury to persons, or damage, throughout the life cycle of military air systems. Its purview includes Airworthiness (but see below), Flight Safety, Policy, Regulation and the apportionment of Resources. It does not address survivability in a hostile environment.

Airworthiness is the ability of an aircraft, or other airborne equipment or system, to be operated in flight and on the ground without significant hazard to aircrew, ground crew, passengers or to third parties, when put to stated uses. It is a technical attribute of materiel throughout its lifecycle. It *does* address survivability, vulnerability and susceptibility in a combat environment, against defined threats.

It can be seen that a sub-airworthy aircraft may meet the criteria for Air Safety, leading many to believe airworthiness regulations can be ignored in order to meet the (lower) Air Safety criteria. In fact, this is MoD's formal position, and lies behind many fatal accidents.[3]

Risk, Tolerability, and As Low As Reasonably Practicable

Risk is the measure which allows safety issues to be compared to how serious they are. It therefore relates to accidents (the events causing harm) rather than hazards (the situations with potential for harm). The basic principle is - avoid the avoidable, manage the unavoidable.

Here we are concerned with safety risks, and specifically risk to life. It is important not to simply state the risk. One must be able to demonstrate what lies beneath and how the risk came about. In other words, was it obvious and if so why was it not mitigated earlier?

Risk assessments must take account of the number of people affected; hence the concept of societal risk (where more than 50 people may be

---

3 For example, C-130 XV179 Inquest, 15 October 2008.

affected), and particularly relevant when considering the Red Arrows.

The Hawk XX179 Service Inquiry report of 29 April 2012 (following the death of Red Arrow Flight Lieutenant Jon Egging on 20 August 2011) recommended that Air Officer Commanding 22 Group:

- *'Develop an effective Unified Risk Register in accordance with Regulatory Article 1210'.*

- *'Conduct a risk assessment to ensure any workload associated risks, for all personnel, are suitably mitigated such that they are Tolerable and ALARP'.*

This neatly captured a number of fundamental principles that were not being adhered to. However, it was too polite. It did not point out that what was being recommended was mandated policy, and very senior staff had already made written declarations that they had assured themselves the policy had been implemented correctly. One solution is complete independence of the report authors (the investigators) from the military chain of command. But whatever the chosen path, robustness is required. *A false declaration was made, resulting in death.*

*

A system is safe when risk has been demonstrated to have been reduced to a level that is Tolerable and As Low As Reasonably Practicable (ALARP); and relevant prescriptive safety requirements have been met, for a system in a given application, in a given operating environment. A risk is ALARP when it has been demonstrated the cost of any further risk reduction, where that cost includes the loss of defence capability as well as the cost of necessary resources, is grossly disproportionate to the benefit obtained from that risk reduction. However, importantly, affordability may not be a consideration.

Tolerability is a willingness to accept risk so as to secure certain benefits, in the confidence that the risk is properly controlled. An intolerable risk can be ALARP, since there may be nothing more that can be done; but servicemen still expected to accept that risk. And for the same risk, in the same system, what is tolerable may differ depending on use. What is tolerable in wartime may not be in peacetime, so extensions in scope, and easements, are common and acceptable. Risk exposure must be proportional to the expected benefit, and can only be fully understood once the ALARP principle has been applied...

Figure 2 - Risk Probability/Severity

The dashed lines are boundaries of acceptability and responsibility. Risks sitting between them may be deemed tolerable, but only if justified on a case-by-case basis as being ALARP. Risks in the Unacceptable region must be mitigated (driven down into the Tolerable if ALARP region) by reducing probability of occurrence and/or severity of harm. Each probability and severity band, and the criteria used, must be defined in the Safety Management Plan; and the decision-maker must be aware of how much risk he can accept, and when to elevate decisions to a higher level.

A risk is ALARP only when the necessary control measures are in place. But in recent years MoD has adopted the concept of 'ALARP (Temporal)', which it uses to justify carrying risks while mitigation is being *considered*, but is not in hand. This is routinely applied to decades-old risks that were understood from the outset, but ignored.

Of crucial import, if the Probability of Occurrence is 100% it is a Certainty, not a Risk, and must be mitigated before proceeding. Failure to do so lies at the heart of most avoidable military aircraft accidents.

To mitigate or not can be guided by a Cost Benefit Analysis. But when viewed within the 'MoD as a business' context it is all too easy to

11

concentrate on cost impacts which are relatively easy to value, to the detriment of safety. Unlike Requirement Scrutiny, these analyses are not carried out from the User's viewpoint; so one must be wary of losing perspective, and concentrate on what really matters.

Safety Cases are required as a means of formally documenting the control of risk, and demonstrating that levels of risk achieved are ALARP. The validity of the argument can only be decided definitively by the courts; and a particular postholder is required to appear (termed the Operating Duty Holder). So far, no court has tested this. In this case, the Coroner was formally requested to by the Bayliss family. She replied indirectly by allowing a subordinate, two ranks below, to appear as a substitute but not answer questions. I discuss his evidence later.

Hazard Log and Risk Register

The Hazard Log is the most important tool for managing safety. It has five parts: system, hazard and accident data, a statement of system safety, and a diary of significant events. A Risk Register is a record of information about identified risks. Generally it includes risk identification, description, category, likelihood, analysis, mitigation, priority, ownership and status.

The aim is to provide an audit trail of how safety issues have been dealt with. Once notified, they must remain in the Log/Register even if dismissed as impossible; because if they turn out to be credible, lessons must be learned and the original decision may have to be defended in court. If probability of occurrence is deemed to be zero, the risk will have a Risk Score (the product of occurrence and severity) of zero, and simply be bottom of a long list. If such a risk should manifest, it is reassessed and may shoot to the top; but in any case all notified hazards and risks are subject to continual review; and must be reviewed regularly by the relevant Safety Committees.

This process is controlled by the Risk Manager, and it is *everyone's* duty to notify him of potential hazards and risks. This obligation is well understood in MoD, but it is common practice to discourage staff from reporting risks because the outcome may be a programme delay or cost increase. Mention of this serves to introduce the RAF's policy, later adopted by the wider MoD, of *savings at the expense of safety*, and confirmed by the Nimrod Review. It, too, lies behind many deaths.

Bow-Ties

These are used to show causal links between sources of risk and consequences. They draw their name from the shape when illustrated:

Figure 3: Bow-Tie analysis

The left side is a simplified fault tree. Conventional Fault Tree Analysis allows the model to be filled with actual numbers about failure probabilities, allowing the calculation of derived probabilities. But in practice this information is seldom available; due mainly to the costs of testing and human influence on the system. Instead, to prevent the focus of the analysis getting bogged down in detail, the Bow-Tie method, originating in the late-70s, simplifies the fault trees, leading to better readability and understanding. They are labour intensive, but so too are the alternatives. The principle of not using numbers has been MoD policy for as long as I can remember; mainly because it can be misleadingly precise, and that apparent precision will often give false assurance. Put another way, it can misrepresent a qualitative assessment as quantitative.

*

While the Red Arrows Bow-Ties are owned by the Commandant Central Flying School (their immediate boss), the Panel noted their construction had been delegated to the squadron's Aircrew Planning Officer, a reserve Squadron Leader. But he had resigned shortly after the accident due to 'the pressures of the role and a progressive increase in responsibilities including overseas tour planning and management, risk register transition to Bow-Tie analysis, management of a new Air Safety reporting programme, and Survival Officer duties'.[4]

Nine months later he had not been replaced, his role temporarily carried out by Flight Lieutenant Stark, while recuperating. The Service Inquiry was withering:

'The importance of the role may not be reflected due to its (Retired Officer) status and that gapping of even a single post in a small busy unit could place further undue pressure on the Team and contribute to a safety related occurrence. In the Panel's opinion, there would be merit in considering the transfer of the position to a Regular Officer liability to ensure continuity in a critical safety area'.

These duties are critical. Three of the four job components mentioned are entirely safety related and properly the job of the Air Safety Management Team - but there wasn't one. His exit created a huge risk.

Making matters worse, the 'Team' at the Central Flying School (CFS) comprised one man; and his was not an established post, meaning he could be removed at any time and it would not be seen as being gapped. So short-handed was CFS, he had been unable to do any work for the Red Arrows. Post-accident, it was he who replaced Flight Lieutenant Stark as Red 3. There was much resistance at CFS to his appointment, due in part to the effect on safety management.[5] The best RAF Personnel could offer the squadron was one part-time officer for 3 months. Pressure was applied, and two others were offered on the same terms. Other safety concerns were 'pushed to the side' as these staff concentrated on Bow-Ties. Too little, far too late.

In his interview with the Panel on 20 June 2018, Air Officer Commanding 22 Group stated this was 'not a constraint at the Red Arrows'. Perhaps more accurately, he also said he had 'enough people, but they were not suitably qualified and experienced'. Disregarding the first claim, the Service Inquiry Panel noted these shortfalls as a Factor in the accident. But nowhere was it mentioned that this situation had been the subject of numerous recommendations following previous fatal accidents.

---

4 XX204 Service Inquiry report, paragraph 1.4.413.

5 Service Inquiry interview with Chief of Staff to Commandant Central Flying School, 12 June 2018.

Given the above, it remains unclear on what evidence the Red Arrows Safety Statement was signed-off, but on 20 July 2018 Air Officer Commanding 22 Group wrote to the Chief of the Air Staff saying the Air Safety Management Team manning was *'compliant'*.[6] This cannot be reconciled with the evidence to, or conclusions of, the Service Inquiry.

*

Regarding *'transition to Bow-Tie'*, a common misconception is that Bow-Ties replace, or serve as, the Risk Register. Bow-Tie is merely a visual representation providing an overview, primarily an aid to carrying out the risk assessment and developing a draft mitigation plan. It must still feed-in to a Risk Register; which in turn must be visible to all stakeholders. The Risk Register is owned and managed by CFS, but they don't have the people to do it.

The Aircrew Planning Officer, during his interview with the Panel:

'We used to have a Unified Risk Register. That was overtaken (and) we now do Bow-Tie risk analysis. At a Delivery Duty Holder Review Group the Risk Register was archived and replaced by the Bow-Ties'.

The Chief of Staff to the Commandant CFS, responsible for providing him with safety assurance and advice, went further:

'I think it's very through in terms of the barriers. I don't think it's very deep in terms of analysis that evaluates the barriers'.

This is a danger sign. These barriers do not exist to compensate for an unsafe condition. Their purpose is to allow you to get to safety when things fail. The perception at the squadron is that they are 'doing' Risk and Safety Management, when in fact they are contributing to one small part of it. Bow-Ties do not present, in any way, an end-to-end process whose output is a mitigated risk. This *'transition'* was actually a dilution of process to compensate for lack of resources; and even then it was immature at 22 Group. For example, the Bow-Ties were not linked to Defence Air Safety Occurrence Reports.

Compliance

The Panel did not discuss the general subject of Risk Management with CFS. It did not ask, for example, *Who approves and who staffs the implementation of mitigation plans?* Nor did it check that the evidence

---

6 AOC22/18/41, 20 July 2022. Red Arrows Safety Statement to the Chief of the Air Staff.

supporting the Tolerable and ALARP claims was documented in the Safety Case. In fact, it didn't mention 'Safety Case' at all, which is sufficient to nullify its investigation. Those responsible were not interviewed. This is reminiscent of the Nimrod Review. The Project Team was criticised for not having a valid Safety Case; ignoring that funding had been withdrawn 15 years before, and teams instructed not to 'do' safety.

There are various Risk Management models, but that shown below is first-rate, reflecting MoD's admirable Defence Standard 00-56 'Safety Management Requirements for Defence Equipment':

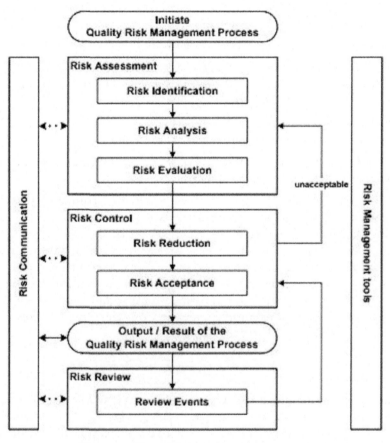

Figure 4: The Risk Management process

If we take each component, from top to bottom, and assess compliance:

- Initiate. MoD is compliant in that a Risk Management process exists, but non-compliant in that refusal to implement it is condoned, and even directed, by senior management.

- Risk Assessment. The bridge between identifying the hazards and the decisions to be made on controlling them. While the inherent risk that killed Jon was Identified, the Analysis and Evaluation were fatally flawed; made worse by the decision that it was sufficient the front seat occupant survive.

- Risk Control. As the mitigation for this risk was repeatedly rejected over a period of decades, no proper Risk Reduction was undertaken. Risk Acceptance, the Tolerable and ALARP statement, was therefore wrong; again exacerbated by the decision that the rear occupant was expendable.

- The Output did not, therefore, comply with legal obligations.

- As the Risk Register passed scrutiny without these failures being identified, the Review Process and Communication failed.

- Evidenced by the Risk Register (e.g. Figures 6a/6b), the Risk Management tools used were inadequate, and poorly used.

At every stage MoD was non-compliant. Thus, serious violations exist across two of the three components of the Service Inquiry - Legal and Technical - and the RAF could not demonstrate Hawk T.1 was airworthy.

*

Risk and safety management are poorly taught in MoD, and it is rare for a project to be allocated a manager for either. The revelation in the Nimrod Review that the project team actually had a Safety Manager shocked many in Air Systems, who realised it was unlikely he was trained correctly. The Review's criticism of him was unfair. To many, it is sufficient to populate the Risk Register. When asked, they will reply *Yes, we have a Risk Register.* But mitigation is an alien concept. Seeing no tangible output when promoted, their ethos permeates and their staff correctly view the subject as unlikely to help their own advancement. This was hinted at by the Service Inquiry President when, at the Inquest in November 2021, he noted that Commandant CFS was *'managing his risks on a daily basis'* - which he then amended to *'or was capturing them'*.

These attitudes lie behind the main root cause of Jon's death, and the associated claims in the Risk Assessments. The Red Arrows had Bow-

Ties, but the Panel confirmed that risks were not being managed correctly, and many obvious ones were not even recorded.

Delegation of safety tasks within MoD

Letters of Delegation serve to delegate the authority for carrying out safety management tasks. A separate delegation exists for Technical and Financial Approval; which, unlike safety, can only be granted to engineers. At the highest level this begins with the Secretary of State, and flows down the management 'pyramid'. A feature of this pyramid is that it is often upside-down.

A Letter of Delegation is not a legal document. It transfers authority, not responsibility. The delegator must ensure the person tasked is suitability competent, provide the necessary resources, and continue to monitor progress. The delegatee must report back on progress and identify shortfalls in achievement or necessary resource. Here, few (if any) delegators had the necessary authority to ensure competence or provide resources, although they could certainly monitor.

The Duty Holder construct [7]

There are three senior levels of accountable individuals for managing risk to life: the Senior, Operating, and Delivery Duty Holders. The Senior Duty Holder is the Top Level Budget Holder or Chief Executive. He appoints the others, who receive and must sign a letter of appointment. In the RAF, for Hawk, the main Duty Holders are:

- Senior Duty Holder (SDH) - Chief of the Air Staff (4-Star), who is required to be able to demonstrate that arrangements are in place to enable any Duty Holder to stop activities in the event that risk to life is no longer considered to be Tolerable and ALARP.

- Operating Duty Holder (ODH) - Air Officer Commanding 22 Group (2-Star), who owns and is accountable for the Air System Safety Case. He/she should record and justify an argument in the Safety Statement that risks are Tolerable and ALARP.

- Aviation System Delivery Duty Holder (DDH) - Commander UK Hawk Wing (a Group Captain), responsible for the safe operation,

---

7 Defence Safety Authority DSA01.2 'Implementation of Defence Policy for Health, Safety and Environmental Protection' - Chapter 3, 'Duty Holding'.

continuing airworthiness and maintenance of RAF (not RN) Hawks. While two ranks below the ODH, he reports directly to him on safety matters.

Note: In 2020 the Red Arrows were transferred to 1 Group. I will use 22 Group, because that was the structure at the time.

With reference to Figure 2, the SDH owns Very High risks ('Unacceptable' region); the ODH High and Medium ('May be Tolerable if ALARP'), and the DDH Low risks ('Broadly Acceptable'). In practice, things are not so clear cut. For example, the SDH holds the public display, societal and reputational risks, but clearly they are not deemed 'Unacceptable'.

One obvious danger here is the Senior Duty Holder being described as the Top Level Budget Holder. Yes he is, but he is also the professional head of the RAF. He is being pulled two ways. Operational vs. political. *Who does he lean towards?* It has been demonstrated many times this is essentially a political post. Appointees are not expected to rock the boat, and to the frustration of servicemen only tend to speak out after retirement. Of course this can be said of any public appointment, but it is especially damaging when directly responsible for tens of thousands of staff, and failure to speak up leads to avoidable deaths.

As a formal element of succession activities, all existing hazards and risks that present a credible risk to life must be reviewed by the incoming Duty Holder to ensure they are content with the level of risk being carried, and the effectiveness of any extant mitigation measures. The downside here is a tendency to assume that *all* risks have been identified and recorded correctly. From there it is one small step, for a busy senior officer, to accept the *status quo*.

This basic construct is nothing new. The primary change has been its weakening since the formation of the Military Aviation Authority in 2010; for example, the periodic review responsibilities placed on 2-Star postholders (e.g. Operating Duty Holders) are now less frequent.

*

As the title suggests, Duty Holders have a duty, which includes the obligation to act conscientiously and with integrity, to exercise their professional judgment to the best of their ability, and pay due care and attention to the matters in their charge. There is a degree of subjectivity involved, and it is common for reasonable people, who are acting honestly and diligently, to have different opinions. When this happens, it is MoD policy that, regardless of specialism, experience or the law, a senior officer cannot be wrong by virtue of rank.

Duty Holders are required to ensure <u>and certify</u> that risks have been mitigated to a level considered Tolerable and ALARP. They must make decisions within their remit, and seek (beg for) help outwith it. With luck, someone at the bottom of the inverted pyramid will have retained and know how to implement the old mandated regulations. At this point, it could be said <u>he</u> becomes the *de facto* accountable decision-maker because, uniquely, he is named in the relevant contracts. The continued use, by some, of these old regulations has saved many lives - and is what allowed staff to give prior notification of the causes of, for example, Hercules XV179 (2005, 10 killed). The warnings were ignored, but even if heeded that is no way to run a Safety Management System.

Only Suitably Qualified and Experienced Persons may be appointed to such posts. But MoD's definition and selection no longer ensures suitability or relevant experience. The assurance once provided by satisfying Grade Descriptions, with advancement based on proven competence, is gone. Critically, and the direct cause of many deaths, is that administrative staff may be appointed to engineering posts and permitted to self-delegate airworthiness and technical approvals.

These and other violations have been confirmed regularly by internal audits. For example, in 2012 Chinook was found to be still suffering from failures reported by the Director of Flight Safety in 1992, despite the RAF Chief Engineer's assurance they had been addressed. And because many core components of this work are centralised activities in MoD, and affected the entire aviation domain, the failing was systemic.

But today, instead of being managed by a few specifically trained specialists, this work is fragmented; a minor task to hundreds of untrained staff. That is not to denigrate these staff. It is an organisational failure. The inevitable duplication is wasteful, and the equally inevitable gaps created are dangerous. Seemingly, no-one understands this. The original decision was conscious, part of the *savings at the expense of safety* policy in the early 1990s. Lack of retention, and short-term postings, means the danger is no longer recognised and has become the norm.

Demonstrating airworthiness - or not

MoD's new Regulatory Set, developed after the creation of the Military Aviation Authority (MAA), is biased towards continuing airworthiness, which applies to individual aircraft, not the type. For example, RA1016 (Continuing Airworthiness Management) and RA1011 (Continuing Airworthiness Management Responsibilities) rather assume type airworthiness has been attained in the first place, and is being maintained; when MoD policy militates against the latter. Continuing Airworthiness Managers have no say in the matter, and almost by definition have never worked in the areas responsible.

But there is another factor. Air Officer Commanding 22 Group stated to the Panel that one *'cannot apply normal Continuing Airworthiness Management rules to Hawk'*. Plainly, if one cannot apply basic, mandated rules, then one must understand why they are no longer adequate. He did not expand, and moved on in August 2020, so this most revealing of comments will probably be filed away - *No further action*.

But what *do* they work to? The Regulatory Set does not include Hawk-specific rules. AOC 22 Group had just admitted that the systemic failings confirmed by the Director of Flight Safety in 1992, and reiterated by the Nimrod Review, remained extant. That, MoD could not demonstrate the airworthiness of any Hawk. No such risk has been elevated to the Senior Duty Holder, the Chief of the Air Staff - whose department signs the Master Airworthiness Reference. A serious conflict of interests exists, and today there is no mechanism that allows those who know the solution to implement it. Similarly, the regulations assume procedures are correct. Here, they were not - and nor were they in 2011 when Sean Cunningham died. Immediately, we have evidence of recurrence.

This is aggravated by, and linked to, the only Defence Standard dedicated to maintaining airworthiness having been cancelled without replacement - another recurring factor in many deaths. Illustrating the point, the MAA Master Glossary incorrectly defines the most important component - Post Design Services, properly defined as 'Maintaining the Build Standard' - and does not even mention 'Build Standard'. Lacking a maintained Build Standard one cannot demonstrate airworthiness, and so cannot justify Service regulated flying except under the most pressing circumstances. That does not apply to the Red Arrows.

Back to basics

While we are discussing a death that occurred some 39 years after the Hawk entered Service, we must regress to assess if known Certainties existed, or were later created, and what action was taken. In this sense, who eliminates Certainties? The overarching process is Safety Management, of which Hazard and Risk Management are part. This begins on Day 1, when what becomes a formal requirement (a training aircraft), and then a capability (Hawk), is simply a Concept - which is the first stage of the Acquisition Cycle.

Initial responsibility is clear, resting with the Directorates of Equipment Capability (DEC), previously the Services' Operational Requirements Branches. They state the 'Requirement' (so why change the name?), and ensure procurers are provided with sufficient information, funding and other resources. I make this distinction because what most of the media and politicians call 'procurement' failures have actually been wholly compromised before procurers got involved. Yes they make errors, but not as often as one is led to believe. Mostly, their role is to salvage what they can from ill-conceived, poorly articulated and under-funded Requirements. While other Service HQ departments know of these Certainties, DECs must play a major role in eliminating them. They don't. This helps explain why the root causes of Jon's death were allowed to develop unchecked.

The transfer and acceptance of residual risk - two case studies

The construct assumes residual risks from the development and production programme have been notified to the Service before formal hand-over and commencement of Service regulated flying. The Duty Holder is seldom the risk creator, and if ill-informed can find himself in an invidious and legally perilous position. Therefore, it is worth studying, by way of two examples, the mechanism by which risks are transferred to, and accepted by Duty Holders.

In 1999 a safety critical risk had become apparent during trials of a new Identification, Friend or Foe system. Failure warnings had not been integrated, so if a failure occurred the crew had no indication they would be seen as 'foes' by allies. On 23 March 2003, Tornado ZG710 was shot down over Kuwait by a US PATRIOT missile battery. Both crew were killed. It wasn't just that the warnings had not been integrated. A written declaration was made that they had, and this had been condoned at 2-Star level despite formal complaints.

In Risk Management terms this was a Class A risk. *Intolerable, and only to be carried under exceptional circumstances*. That is, it was held at the time by the Chief of Defence Procurement (4-Star), who was fully aware

22

because he had rejected the complaints.

Each time, the complainant went back and asked both to reaffirm their rulings. In other words *Do you really understand what you are saying?* Both repeated their decisions.[8] The risk was transferred to the Chief of the Air Staff, but without him being informed.

But in my experience these very senior officers do not attend hand-overs between the project office and Service. The closest I have known is a 1-Star Commodore RN who had shown personal interest in a Certainty (aircrew hearing damage). When informed it had been mitigated to Class C/ALARP and asked to confirm it was Tolerable (i.e. he would accept transfer), he chose to fly the first sortie himself. That cleared the Certainty, and is how the process is meant to work.

But a non-engineer cancelled the mitigation of two other Class A risks which the Commodore had been content were being mitigated to Class C. As with the Chief of the Air Staff (above), his successor did not know that, in accepting the aircraft, he was taking on these critical risks to life. The day before Tornado ZG710 was shot down the risks manifested exactly as predicted, and seven Sea King crew were killed in a mid-air collision over the Northern Arabian Gulf.[9]

In both cases, those responsible were easily identifiable. None have been interviewed, and the families await action; although to his credit Sir Roger Gale MP tried to press on the Sea King case and commissioned a major report. It was submitted to the chairman of the Defence Select Committee, who took no action.[10]

*

A further defence in depth exists when the design is brought Under Ministry Control. The Service <u>must</u> attend the Transfer Meeting; which involves, for example, tabling the Certificates of Design and ensuring the Aircraft Document Set is valid. That is, it sets the latest airworthiness baseline. An extensive checklist is laid down, and core items <u>must</u> be compliant. Only the Chair, a civilian engineer, is permitted to grant waivers, and only on sub-items. (A further example of the inverted

---

8 Letters XD1(304), 15 December 2000 and 10 January 2001, and CDP 117/6/7, 19
   November 2001 and 13 December 2001.

9 'Breaking the Military Covenant' (David Hill, 2018).

10 E-mail Sir Roger Gale MP/Rory Stewart MP (Chair of Defence Select Committee), 14
   January 2015 11:14, enclosing report 'Contributory Factors'.

pyramid). Another defence is that a significant financial milestone payment is always attached to this, acting as an incentive. In this way, residual technical and safety risks hitherto owned by the company are formally transferred.

These principles apply here. The Red Arrows Risk Register, published after Sean Cunningham's death in 2011, reveal Class A risks remained from before Service regulated flying was approved in 1979. For example, lack of front seat Command Eject, discussed later. The records of the transfer and hand-over must be retained; but MoD has confirmed they were not, resulting in a loss of corporate knowledge.

*

Okay, I've set out the problem. What to do? Let us take the most obvious Certainty in military aviation - airworthiness will not have been maintained. As senior staff (including DECs) allow this and have persistently refused to budge, the first action an individual project or programme manager must take is to stabilise the Build Standard, which is the basis of functional safety. This will resurrect (or generate in the first place) the Hazard Log, Risk Register and Safety Case.

This has always been a risk, but when did it become a Certainty? In 1987 the RAF promulgated the aforementioned policy dubbed *'savings at the expense of safety'*.[11] Over the next five or so years airworthiness, and safety management in general, were run down; and was ultimately prohibited in January 1993 by simply removing resources, forcing specialist staff to seek other posts. Gradually, over many years, matters improved. But they have not returned to normal. Gaps that were created in (e.g.) Build Standards, and hence Safety Cases, were not closed.

Occasionally a programme manager would, coincidentally, have knowledge of what was needed, and quietly slip it into a much larger contract. But such coincidences are rare, and there is a direct correlation with many accidents. The day someone accountable is in the witness box explaining himself, is the day the system will start to recover.

None of the aforegoing was mentioned in the Service Inquiry report or at the Inquest. Yet it explains most of the underlying factors. The solution is to *Do what you're meant to be doing.*

---

11 Letter D/DDSS11(RAF)/48/9, 30 November 1987.

Safety Cases

The risk creator is responsible for proving that activities are going to be tolerably safe. To this end, MoD mandates the establishment and maintenance of Safety Cases. Their purpose is to *(inter alia)*:

- Document evidence that the Safety Requirements are being met, and that all identified risks are Tolerable and ALARP.

- Demonstrate that any activities underway at that time (including tests or trials) can be carried out safely.

- Describe clearly the evidence and arguments used to justify the safety of the system, so that agreement can be reached on the validity of the claim of tolerable safety.

They must consider five questions:

1. What are we looking at? (System description).

2. What could go wrong? (Hazard identification and analysis).

3. How bad could it be? (Risk assessment).

4. What has been or can be done about it? (Risk and ALARP appraisal, mitigation and acceptance).

5. What if it happens? (Tolerability, emergency and contingency).

And should answer these for each of the uses defined in the Statement of Operating Intent and Usage, and for each Build Standard. It follows that the former must be up-to-date and the latter maintained, and any change reflected in the Safety Case. They should contain an explicit safety argument, underpinned by evidence, around which one can base audit and airworthiness recommendations.

It is the sole responsibility of MoD to determine the tolerability of any reduction in safety levels deemed necessary when operating under emergency/conflict or classified role conditions. This does not apply to the Red Arrows, but acts as a reminder that MoD must be at least proactive. BAe Systems may be the Design Authority for Hawk, but the caveat is that they, and aircraft equipment suppliers, must always be under contract to maintain the Build Standard, which includes the Safety Case. If they are not, there will be an incomplete audit trail.

The Safety Case is condensed in the Safety Case Report, which sets out residual risks and is updated at key points such as when the form, fit, function or use changes. (*'Residual'* implies that Hazard and Risk Management has been conducted in the first place). It is defined as:

'The means by which the Project demonstrates that all of the safety issues relating to a project have been brought to a condition appropriate for the stage in the life cycle'.

Valid Safety Cases are therefore a tangible output of an effective Safety Management System. Hawk didn't have one. Nor is there evidence that any of these data depositories (Risk Register, Hazard Log, Safety Case) were in any way integrated (electronically linked). Of course, this was impossible when Hawk was being developed, but MoD project offices have had integrated IT systems, and the necessary software, since July 1996. These are systemic failures.

*

A key appointment at the outset is the Independent Safety Auditor (ISA); to audit both MoD and its Contractors, and make airworthiness recommendations to the Project Director. Importantly, individual Design Authority Safety Case policies must be agreed with the ISA. This prior agreement of the 'Safety Case Boundary' is crucial to ensure cost control, and that the Safety Case covers what the ISA anticipated.

The ISA must be acceptable to both, be independent of both, and be competent in three distinct domains - technical, auditing and behavioural. For Air Systems, MoD's practice is to appoint what was the Aeroplane and Armament Experimental Establishment at Boscombe Down, now part of defence contractor QinetiQ. On aircraft programmes, Boscombe defines a Safety Case as:

'The study of an aircraft or item of aircraft equipment to identify and show acceptability (or otherwise) of the potential hazards associated with it. The Safety Case provides a reasoned argument supported by evidence, establishing why the Design Authority is satisfied that the aircraft is safe to use and fit for its intended purpose'.

This is excellent because it mentions both aircraft and aircraft equipment, which MoD makes provision for and manages in separate ways. Also, it makes clear the Design Authority's responsibility. I cannot bring myself to repeat MoD's misuse of the term 'Design Organisation'. That is an <u>accreditation</u>, and but one prerequisite to being <u>appointed</u> as a Design Authority. One can be a Design Approved Organisation, but lack the basic infrastructure and expertise to be a Design Authority. In fact, one can be the former and yet never be awarded an MoD contract. But an appointment as the latter means the company has been appraised against more stringent criteria, and been granted significant delegation by MoD. I stress this, because failure to understand and apply the associated regulations has led to many deaths, including Jon's.

*

When development reaches the stage where Boscombe considers an aircraft type is airworthy, at a stated Build Standard, it makes its *recommendations*. If the Project Director accepts them, they are issued as a *statement* to the Service. Its content is *mandated* upon the Service, and it becomes the Release to Service (the Master Airworthiness Reference). Thus, an inviolable audit trail is created, and must be maintained, between Statement of Operating Intent and Usage, Build Standard, Safety Case, and Release to Service. The desired output is the evidence underpinning the decision to conduct Service regulated flying.

Every Limitation in the Release must be traceable to a potential hazard within the Safety Case, or to a source that shows clearly that it has been introduced for other reasons, such as aircraft husbandry. By definition, then, a valid Safety Case is a prerequisite to declaring airworthiness and authorising Service regulated flying; which is important here because in the Sean Cunningham case the MAA's witness at the trial of Martin-Baker claimed to the media that the lack of a Safety Case for Hawk was irrelevant. Here, most 'Limitations' in the Hawk Release are not traceable in this way, partly because many are not Limitations at all.

If for any reason the Safety Case becomes invalid (here, for example, through realising that the aircraft handling characteristics were no longer understood), then a decision can be made by the Operating Duty Holder (2-Star) to carry the risk. But only if it remains, or can be made, Tolerable and ALARP; say by curtailing certain manoeuvres. (What the RAF did post-accident). And any invalidity often manifests as components of the Aircraft Document Set not being reconcilable.

If invalidity persists, or occurrences thereof increase, that is a major warning sign of systemic failures. Flying becomes increasingly difficult to justify. This is seldom black and white. The main Duty Holders are often remote from the coalface, the point at which a risk becomes intolerable may not be clear, and there is the operational imperative to consider. Only in hindsight do they realise that aircrew (and passengers) have been nibbled to death by ducks.

In every case I have studied, not only was it patently obvious that Service regulated flying could not be justified, but statements and/or warnings to that effect had been ignored. The classic example is Chinook HC Mk2,

27

prior to the Mull of Kintyre accident in 1994. Boscombe firmly stated that the aircraft was not airworthy, among other things citing *'positively dangerous'* safety critical engine control software implementation. Controller Aircraft (a 3-Star) concurred, <u>mandating</u> upon the RAF that the aircraft only had a ground training and familiarisation clearance. He was ignored by the (more junior) Assistant Chief of the Air Staff, who gave approval to fly the aircraft, falsely stating that it was airworthy. If this were an isolated case it would be negligence. But taken with the formal warnings received on his first day in post (August 1992), this was reckless endangerment of aircrew and passengers.

*

At the Inquest in November 2021, under questioning by Jon's father Michael, the Service Inquiry President said he had examined the Air System Safety Case and *'all parts were valid'*. Yet his own report listed (conservatively) 24 Factors, 7 Observations and 22 Recommendations relating to anomalies in the Safety Case; and between it and the rest of the Aircraft Document Set.

'All parts were valid'? That is not the same as all the required parts being present and correct. A Safety Case that has just been initiated may have a pretty cover and an opening narrative describing the subject, but nothing else; and those *'parts'* may be *'valid'* (well-grounded, cogent, meaningful). But the Service Inquiry report certainly does not describe a valid Safety Case. It describes one in complete disarray.

The Coroner asked the President:

'In terms of the documentation was the aircraft considered airworthy?'

'Yes, the aircraft was considered airworthy and serviceable in the period prior to the accident, and in the immediate period before the aircraft took off for the final sortie. And it was assumed that the aircraft was serviceable throughout as the pilot did not report a malfunction'.

This was carefully worded, bounding the timeframe. The person who *'considered'* XX204 airworthy was a junior officer at RAF Scampton; relying entirely on the firm, binding statement in the Release to Service that the Aircraft Document Set was complete and valid. It was in disrepair and incoherent. The Release was invalid, because the primary underpinning evidence, a valid Safety Case reflecting the Red Arrows concept of use, and based on a maintained Build Standard, did not exist.

*

The initial development of Safety Cases, by industry, is managed quite well. Matters break down later, due to not treating Safety Management as a through-life process - a mindset that manifested itself in the decision to deny the Red Arrows an Air Safety team.

It is for MoD to *demonstrate* an aircraft is airworthy. It could not in 2011 after Sean Cunningham was killed, and despite the failures being known, it still couldn't in 2018. Is that seven year gap acceptable? No reasonable person would believe so. However, if one wishes to be pedantic, to anyone below the Assistant Chief of the Air Staff the Hawk *was* airworthy, because he signed to say it was. But only one of those arguments will stand up in court.

4. The accident flight

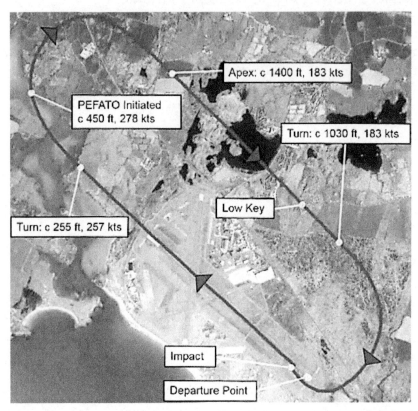

Figure 5: The manoeuvre conducted by Flight Lieutenant Stark *(MoD)*

It can be seen the return leg is not parallel to the runway - caused by wind, and making the required final turn tighter. In evidence, one pilot confirmed that guideline heights and speed assume the flight through Low Key is downwind, and have to be adjusted accordingly. This is a virtual position, or reference point, abeam the Initial Aiming Point for the landing; which is one third along the runway, appearing as a 'line' (a roadway) across the runway. At this point landing gear is UP, but intent has been called to Air Traffic Control when, in a brief final call, the pilot confirms he has identified the Aiming Point.

Flight Lieutenant Stark's case was that he had not been told the minimum height guidance to begin his final turn was 1400 feet. This had been introduced into FTP3225H, the Hawk T.1 Training Manual, seven weeks before the accident:

'The minimum height at which the 300 feet "contract" might still be met is about 1400ft assuming a perfectly flown gliding turn with the gear lowered just after half way around the turn'.

Hitherto no minimum was given; and afterwards it was changed to 1700 feet. The Service Inquiry report did not say where the 1400 feet came from, or why it was changed again to 1700 feet after the accident, although one can glean possibilities. While it explored FTP3225H in detail, its report also omitted the following, without which some might infer Stark erred:

'I was aware that this height was Qualified Flying Instructor (QFI) guidance to students and if the Practice Forced Landing (PFL) gate was not met then the QFI knew that the PFL contract was unlikely to be met, after about 180 degrees of glide turn, for the average pilot. This guidance was not, however, written in any document but did appear in unofficial QFI notes. It was finally included in the January 2018 issue [of FTP3225H] after consultation with Hawk handling Subject Matter Experts (and practiced in the simulator by myself to validate). This is why it is specifically caveated as "a guide" rather than a specific minima or contract'.[12]

It remains unclear what formal verification process the amendment went through. The report would have benefited from a comment by the Publications Authority, but it would seem none were spoken to by the Panel.

---

12 E-mail 100 Squadron Hawk T1 Central Flying School Agent to Service Inquiry President, 10 September 2018 18:03.

5. The accident investigation

The aim of accident investigation is to bring to light potential or actual failures, either human or technical. The objective is to establish and record all the relevant facts without distortion, argue their relationship to the accident, and identify its cause(s) in order that changes may be brought about to prevent recurrence. It is a search for the truth; but always recognising that the search does not always deliver certainty.

The investigation is therefore an essential component of air safety. It must find out the reason for any shortcoming it uncovers, regardless of its contribution to the accident. Failure to do so promotes recurrence; and an inadequate report, in any regard, nullifies the investigation. The purpose is not to identify in the report those responsible, although that is often unavoidable. It must be accepted that there doesn't always have to be someone to blame. Unforeseen and unimagined things do happen, and errors of judgment can be made innocently and in good faith. However, it is essential that if anyone has erred this be recognised and corrected through, for example, retraining.

The investigation team must be independent, strictly impartial, and must be allowed to investigate and report without fear or favour and free from pressure to modify their opinion. They must be honest, and possess a high degree of skill and application that will ensure no possible aspect is overlooked, while being able to identify and eliminate false leads and attempts to disrupt the investigation.

While there may be many interested parties, the only people who can formally investigate are those paid to do so. Therefore *Who pays the investigator?* is the key question when determining independence.[13] MoD defines independence as having separate management chains, but does not specify the degree of separation. Here, the Convening Authority, who was also the regulator and arbiter, sat only one below (e.g.) the professional head of the RAF. Therefore, no MoD investigation or inquiry can possibly meet this internationally accepted criteria.

At the Inquest, in 2021, the Coroner confirmed:

'The Defence Safety Authority (DSA), whilst independent from the RAF and

---

13 'Safety Is No Accident' (W.H. Tench, 1985).

indeed a single service authority, is an agency in the Ministry of Defence and reports to the Secretary of State for Defence. The DSA is therefore the investigating authority within the very department of State which may be held responsible for any breaches found'.

Divergence - cause of accident and cause of death

A Service Inquiry Panel looks at cause of the accident. Cause of death is the sole domain of the Coroner (or the Procurator Fiscal in Scotland). The two are complementary. There is overlap, but better that than gaps.

The Service Inquiry was required to identify factors which, if removed from the entire sequence, would have the prevented the accident. These are termed root causes. For example, a question which must always be asked and answered is - *Should the aircraft have been flying at all?*

Here, an important distinction exists. The pilot survived, and Jon's family wanted to know why *he* didn't. Therefore, the points of divergence had to be identified, and the following asked:

1. Was there any reason why Jon should not have been in the aircraft?
2. Was there anything that could have saved him?
3. Were these factors known beforehand, when, why was nothing done, and who made that decision?

Any divergences will then be root causes of death, but not the accident, and should become the focus of the Coroner's Inquest. Here they did <u>not</u>, and combined with lack of independence and failure to establish and record all relevant facts, nullified both investigation and Inquest.

There were two main points of divergence. Jon being incorrectly classified as Supernumerary Crew; and the pilot ejecting successfully. I later devote a section to each.

The Service Inquiry [14]

The Service Inquiry convened on 28 March 2018. The Convening Authority was Director General Defence Safety Authority. The Panel comprised a Royal Navy Commander as President, an RAF pilot and an Army engineer. A legal advisor from the Military Aviation Authority was appointed to assist. A team of investigators from the Defence

---

14 XX204 Service Inquiry Report DSA/SI/02/18, 24 April 2019.

Accident Investigation Branch conducted the engineering investigation of the physical evidence at the scene. (They should not be confused with the Air Accidents Investigation Branch who, in civil accidents, look at all engineering matters including type certification and airworthiness).

Inter alia, the Panel was required to investigate, and if possible determine, the cause of the *accident*, and the serviceability of the aircraft and relevant equipment. It was required to assess and report on:

Causal Factors (Root Causes) - which, in isolation or in combination with other causal factors and contextual details, lead directly to the accident. Lacking a full engineering investigation, the Panel identified only one - the application of g-force in the three seconds prior to the initiation of the go-around. (The act of terminating an approach by applying full power, rolling wings level, and climbing). The aircraft stalling was coincident with the go-around, not a consequence of it.

Nevertheless, this, and the flight profile, did not solely explain why the accident happened, as at any stage the pilot could have terminated the exercise by initiating a go-around. My interpretation is that the Panel thought this an 'unintentional act' - an error of judgment at most.

Contributory Factors - which make the accident more likely to happen, but do not directly cause it. Therefore, if a contributory factor had been removed from the accident sequence, the accident may still have occurred. The Panel identified nine:

1. Red Arrows Practice Forced Landing and PEFATO currency requirements leading to the potential for skill fade.

2. The carriage of Circus in the aircraft during the conduct of Practice Forced Landings initiated below 1000 feet Above Ground Level.

3. The aircraft's height and lateral spacing at the start of the final turn.

4. The pilot's lack of awareness regarding the amended PEFATO guidance in FTP3225H. (The Hawk T.1/1A Handling Manual).

5. The lack of an aircraft stall warning capability.

6. High Angle of Bank and excessive Rate of Descent.

7. The pilot's working routine was affecting his morale, not allowing him sufficient time for rest or consolidation.

8. Pilot fatigue.

9. Distraction during critical stage of flight.

Aggravating Factors - which make the final outcome of the accident worse but do not cause or contribute to the accident. Therefore, in the absence of the aggravating factor, the accident would still have occurred.

1. Jon's lack of experience to independently initiate his own ejection.
2. The lack of a front seat-initiated Command Ejection system.

This correctly identified a point of divergence.

Other Factors - which are none of the above and, whilst shown to have been present, played no part in the accident but are noteworthy in that they could contribute to or cause a future accident.

1. Red Arrows general currency requirements resulting in skill fade.
2. Non-recording of individual Practice Forced Landing profiles could result in them remaining unpracticed.
3. The lack of a training requirement for a stall recovery in a glide.
4. The lack of appropriate Quality Assurance.
5. The Red Arrows were not using the mandated forms and methodology for recording, calculating and informing the basic Weight and Moment or the Current Operating Weight.
6. Inaccurate Weight and Moment and Centre of Gravity calculations.
7. Insufficient authorisation detail regarding sortie content when carrying inexperienced passengers/Supernumerary Crew.
8. The lack of Circus simulator training.
9. The lack of a formal syllabus for shakedown sorties.
10. The lack of clarity regarding Supernumerary Crew status.
11. The lack of clarity of handling guidance following an EFATO.
12. The lack of guidance for increasing Angle of Bank above 45° and the associated relationship with the required increase in speed.
13. The utilisation of the standard go-around technique could, with a fine stall margin, result in an aircraft stalling.
14. The conduct of practice malfunctions in an aircraft following the completion of complex emergency drills in a simulator.

15. The lack of a Cockpit Voice Recorder constrained the investigation.

16. The generation of increased workload and associated pressure on the Red Arrows Qualified Flying Instructors.

17. The combination of induced pressure and lack of engineers.

18. The lack of Bow-Tie supporting evidence to formulate an overall risk assessment and provide understanding of implications.

19. Failure to record risks and articulate associated mitigation relating to the requirement for Circus and Supernumerary Crew.

20. The lack of a permanently established Air Safety team.

21. Incorrect information contained within the Aircrew Manual.

Observations - issues identified that are worthy of note to improve working practices, but do not relate to the accident being investigated and which could not contribute to or cause future accidents.

1. Differences between the three Hawk T.1 squadrons in the frequency requirements for core handling exercises.

2. For non-primary tasks electronic authorisation was not as robust as manually written authorisation.

3. Electronic authorisation sheets could be amended without either the authoriser or pilot's knowledge.

4. Limited regulatory advice regarding electronic documentation.

5. Hawk simulator reports should record an individual's performance, including appropriate advice.

6. The failure to lock seat harnesses during critical stage of flight.

7. Delays in the provision of key documentation had the potential to significantly delay Service Inquiry progress.

8. A failure to make Accident Data Recorder calibration data readily available hinders progress with assessing essential evidence and generating an early understanding of the incident flight.

9. The importance of the Aircrew Planning Officer role may not be reflected due to its Full Time Reserve Service status, and that gapping of even a single post in a small busy unit could place further undue pressure on the Team.

10. The Delivery Duty Holder's Air Safety register appeared to be more

of a personal record rather than a formal decision register.

*

The Panel's recommendations arose from these Factors (but not the Observations). They are discussed in advance with Duty Holders to ensure all agree they are achievable. (Although MoD does not explain what happens if no postholder agrees to own a recommendation, or if what he agrees to is so diluted it is meaningless). It is the role of the Delivery Duty Holder to track progress. As there were three distinct Hawk operators (1 Group, 22 Group and 736NAS), it was agreed Air Officer Commanding 22 Group would lead.

It will become clear that what is entirely missing from the process (Service Inquiry and Inquest) is an assessment of these Factors and Observations against the *cause of death*. For example, Other Factor #19 is an Aggravating, and arguably Causal Factor. Others are prerequisites to conducting Service regulated flying.

Regarding Other Factors #5 & 6, it was stated in evidence that the Red Arrows had a dispensation not to record weight and moment in the aircraft MF700 (engineering records). Similarly, the Hawk Integrated Operational Support contractor.[15] So, the centre of gravity assurance was not available to the pilot when he signed-out the aircraft. (It was not asked why anyone would approve such a thing).

Regarding Observations #9 & 10, the Panel omits the associated culture and behavioural failings, and that they clearly affect the entire RAF. Most importantly, every Observation describes a fundamental breakdown of the Safety Management System. As they are 'only' Observations, with no associated recommendations, the scale of this most serious of failings is glossed over.

*

The Convening Order states:

'During the course of your investigations, should you identify a potential conflict of interest between the Convening Authority and the Inquiry, you are to pause work and take advice from your DSA Legal Advisor and Director General Defence Safety Authority'.

This differs markedly from previous policy:

---

15 Service Inquiry interview with Red Arrows Junior Engineering Officer, 15 May 2018.

'The President is to report immediately to the convening officer if it becomes apparent that the conduct of <u>an officer superior to himself</u> will be called into question'.

It was known that MoD could not demonstrate airworthiness, and so the Defence Safety Authority knew it would be judging its own case. There was no pause. That is not to criticise the Panel. It can never be known what its original report said, as it is subject to 'review' at every level. Interference is common. This can take many forms; from starting again with a new Panel, to more subtle hints. The President of one RAF Service Inquiry into a Tornado mid-air collision in July 2012:

'In the end, the Director General [Military Aviation Authority] *didn't actually agree with me (as it would have more than likely ended up in a 2-Star being taken to court)... but I still believe that more sensible mitigations could have been done and therefore the risk* [of collision] *was not ALARP'.*

It is difficult to understand precisely what is expected of the President. Some seem to delve deeply, perhaps because they have an innate understanding of the subject. But, for example, when asked for help by a bereaved family the President of the 2003 Sea King ASaC Mk7 mid-air (Iraq, 7 killed) declined to comment, saying the technical investigation of the recovered wreckage was not part of his Board of Inquiry and so he lacked involvement. The two reports (and hence the evidence to the Inquest) were contradictory, and no attempt was made to reconcile them. That nullified the entire investigation and Inquest.

It is almost unknown for a Panel to seek expert advice on the systemic failures they note, and even rarer for them to be described as such. This is partly a cultural failing, and partly because they are discouraged from pointing out repeat failures. The deeper truth only emerges once the reports can be independently assessed. This is a case in point.

Summary of factors [16]

The Panel concluded that the aircraft stalled during its final approach, with insufficient height to recover. The Accident Data Recorder (ADR) revealed it experienced a roll reversal and a distinct drop of the right wing; the latter the first indication (in the recording) of a stall. Speed was approximately 146 knots, having reduced from 150 knots in the preceding second. The ADR revealed no indications of positive stall

---

16 XX204 Service Inquiry Report, Section 1.4.

recovery actions being applied prior to the wing drop, therefore it was unclear if the pilot had recognised the approaching stall.

The Panel reiterated that a pilot conducting a Practice Forced Landing at low altitude, particularly when close to the minimum speed without an indication of stall margin (the difference between stall onset and stall), would have inadequate warning, and could stall the aircraft with insufficient height to recover. XX204 was flown at the minimum recommended speed and close to Maximum All Up Weight; and due to the geometry of the manoeuvre (i.e. the final turn was too tight) the pilot required a high Angle of Bank and increased g-force to achieve runway alignment. These events, combined with a high Rate of Descent, resulted in a stall. (The pilot was aware of his All Up Weight and consciously entered the PEFATO at 10 knots higher than his minimum).

Regarding weight, Air Officer Commanding 22 Group confirmed:

'We're not entirely convinced that we know exactly what weight these aircraft are, with the paint jobs they've had over time'.

This is a well-known factor in aircraft support, his comment suggesting a lack of resources and/or Suitably Qualified and Experienced Persons - both of which he voiced concern over. Paint is very heavy, and stripping and re-applying it time-consuming and expensive; so many layers are often allowed to build up. (I recall the endurance of one helicopter being extended by 15 minutes by a paint strip, which is utterly crucial in, for example, Search and Rescue). In a fast jet, such unrecorded variations would affect handling, and the minimum speed for (e.g.) Practice Forced Landings. In part, this explained changes in advice given to pilots; but this was not always promulgated in a timely fashion, or in the correct place.

The Air Warfare Centre and QinetiQ undertook flight tests. With no stores fitted, the stall was characterised primarily by a clearly defined wing drop of up to 30 degrees, with a g-break (a sudden loss of lift at or near the stall). But with the smoke pod fitted, the stall was less clearly defined, with a less distinct wing drop and g-break. Sometimes, the most obvious sign a stall had occurred was a sudden and not always immediately apparent wash-off in speed of several knots. In the Panel's opinion, the 4-knot reduction in speed within one second may have been associated with the aircraft entering the stalled condition. It was implied that this had not been identified during previous trials.

Importantly, the Panel's report confirmed the aircraft was flying under an invalid Release to Service - although it didn't spell this out. Interpretation was required.

Common factors

The Panel made 25 recommendations. It would probably at least suspect most were mandated policy. But in court the President confirmed he had only looked at the two most recent Red Arrows accidents, both in 2011, and that his recommendations *'didn't track from previous recommendations'*. That is, his report omitted that the following factors and observations were also recorded in the previous accident, to XX177 on 8 November 2011:

- The accident was avoidable.
- No common training objectives, lack of continuation training, and failure to record training.
- Improper recording of maintenance actions.
- Red Arrows adopted different procedures to other squadrons.
- Safety Case not appropriate to function and use.
- Risks not ALARP.
- Inaccuracy and ambiguity of, and between, publications; and failure by MoD to disseminate publications and information.
- Quality Assurance and authorisation failures compromised safety.
- Perceived pressure arising from overworked aircrew/increased tempo/lack of resources (especially Air Safety staff).

It is impossible for anyone reading both reports to miss these commonalities. Omitting (or deleting) this must have been deliberate.

The recommendations were aimed at eight individuals, the effect being to spread responsibility so thinly that recurrence is inevitable. What was needed was a single recommendation to the Secretary of State - *It's happened again. Set up a legal review into these long-term systemic failings.*

Warning signs

While the risk of stalling during the final turn were well known, the Hawk T.1 did not have artificial stall warning to allow the pilot to take corrective action prior to onset. Lacking this, the Panel thought it unlikely a pilot would instinctively choose to unload the aircraft (reduce the lift) to recover from such a nose low attitude with high Angle of Bank, and then have the awareness and control to be able to stay clear of the stall. When mental processing time was considered, the minimum height needed would increase further. The Panel concluded it was impossible for the aircraft to recover from the stall.

Consequently, it recommended that Air Officer Commanding 22 Group, the Operating Duty Holder, should investigate the incorporation of a warning capability in the Hawk T.1. At the Inquest, the President was asked by the Coroner when stall warners were first available. MoD's QC, Mr Pleeth, interjected saying *'Group Captain Jackson will be able to explain these details'*. But Jackson later refused, and being the final witness this meant the question was never answered.

Pilot fatigue and secondary duties

A major red flag in the report is a section discussing the work routine imposed on Red Arrows pilots, causing fatigue; the risk being it leads to pilot error. Two Hawk accidents are relevant - XX249 on 28 September 2001; and XX193 in which both crew were killed on 22 October 1999. The next available reference is the Red Arrows Risk Register, an Exhibit in the XX177 (Sean Cunningham) Service Inquiry report of 2012. It contains two fatigue-related risks: (1) CFIT-PILINC/02 - 'Cumulative Fatigue', and (2) STFBS/01 - 'Fatigue'.

Hitherto, the probability of occurrence was assessed as 'remote':

'Likely to occur one or more times in 10 years, but not more than once a year'.[17]

Post-XX177, in 2012 this was revised to 'improbable':

'Unlikely to occur in 10 years'.

The worst possible outcome is recorded as: *'Loss of aircraft and death of pilot'.* Passengers are not mentioned. What mitigation was proposed to achieve 'improbable'?

'Fatigue management as detailed in Red Arrows Air Safety Management Plan. Crew Duty Time. Programmed rest days. No more than 6 days work without

---

17 Regulatory Instruction MAA RI/02/11 DG, Annex D, paragraph 3. One could argue these definitions are too simplistic, and indeed they are contradicted elsewhere in MoD's regulations which require the criteria to be set for each programme in its Risk Management Plan.

a day off.

As the risks were declared ALARP in 1999 and 2001, the implication is these simple changes were not thought possible before 2012.

The XX177 Service Inquiry noted that the Red Arrows Display Directive *'omitted a number of items, such as fatigue'*, but made no recommendation.

*

Originally, secondary duties were intended to be minor, to help the day-to-day running of (all) squadrons. Gradually, with successive 'efficiency measures' they have become burdensome, and in many cases the *de facto* major role and worthy of a full-time post. The reality is that they are now used to compensate for deficiencies in resource and personnel, denying pilots time to study and consolidate. What was once 'surge' is now considered the normal tempo. This can be said of most of MoD, with *'no more than six days...'* an unheard of luxury to many. The problem is 'creep'. *Oh, you're managing, here's another 20 hours work a week.* And then you suddenly fall off the cliff. Quite the worst case I have written evidence of is a line manager e-mailing a critically ill subordinate, telling him to commence a new task, work through the Xmas holiday period, and complete it against a strict deadline.[18] This was deemed acceptable by the entire management chain, up to and including 4-Star. A few young, healthy pilots are the tip of an iceberg.

The Panel acknowledged Flight Lieutenant Stark's secondary duties were the most onerous amongst aircrew. For example, he had to ensure the IT worked, sandwiches were made, and the kitchen tidy. The result was toxic. At the Inquest, one witness confirmed that these duties became more taxing as the build-up to the display season intensified, to the point where one began to *'question one's ability as a pilot'*. The Panel concluded the pilot's *'work routine was a Contributory Factor'*.

One explanation offered to the Panel was that secondary duties served to prepare the pilots for what to expect *'on the road'* during the display season, when there are no support staff. *Savings at the expense of safety?*

*

Related to this, the Red Arrows are now the closest there is to a 'traditional' squadron, with all-military aircrew and engineers. Whereas, others are now mostly supported by outsourced maintenance contracts

---

18 E-mail DCCRM, 23 December 2002 11:27 'DS2 SIRG'.

- widely recognised as one of MoD's most damaging policies, not least because it removed the natural recruitment grounds for suitably qualified and experienced people. This brings its own problems, one being the squadron does not have an Engineering Wing. So, the Senior Engineering Officer is also the *de facto* Officer Commanding Engineering and Supply. Also, being isolated from other Hawk squadrons means they must, for example, rely disproportionately on RAF Valley, on the other side of England and Wales, for resources that others expect to be local. In short, the RAF's flagship squadron is poorly served, which may seem odd to an outsider.

This was put well by Air Officer Commanding 22 Group, Air Vice Marshal Warren James, when describing them as an *'expeditionary unit'*. Elsewhere in MoD such units warrant, and are provided with, additional resources. But the Red Arrows, and 22 Group in general, did not benefit in this way. In fact, the AOC confirmed that one of the reasons for changing his Group's name from 22 Training Group to 22 Group in January 2018 was the perception it was *'only a training Group'* and on the *'bottom rung'* of the RAF ladder. This certainly explains much.

*

Central Flying School offered an intriguing alternative view. The Commandant's Chief of Staff, a former Harrier and display pilot, discussing the squadron's training and display programme:

'I don't think their regime, looking at the programme, is particularly stretching at all. I think it's quite reasonable'.[19]

He was talking of their tangible output; and to this one must add the other flying tasks placed upon them, such as ceremonial fly pasts, which are not classified as displays. And, especially, the undoubted pressure they are under to deliver a full complement of nine aircraft:

'I think they are under a lot of pressure to deliver (a 9-ship) each time, albeit a message is constantly we don't need to. I think anybody would be kidding themselves if they would readily accept an 8-ship'.

On secondary duties specifically:

'I think it's quite manageable. I think they get shielded from quite a bit

---

19 Service Inquiry interview with Chief of Staff to Commandant Central Flying School, 12 June 2018.

compared to other trainee units, other front-line units. I don't think their workload outside the cockpit is any greater, and I don't think it has an impact on their ability to do their job. I don't think their (secondary duties) are overly burdensome or impact on their ability to do the job or their fatigue stress levels'.

This painted a quite different picture, and was certainly 'off message'. The Panel disregarded this entirely - or perhaps it was removed from their report, one of many areas where it does not set out all the evidence. Instead, it presented total accord.

(It was announced in May 2022 that the Red Arrows would display as a 7-ship during the forthcoming season. Three pilots had left in quick succession. That might seem careless, and perhaps an internal review will make recommendations to prevent recurrence. Or perhaps not, given the reasons for two of them are recurrences, with the reputational risk sitting with the Chief of the Air Staff).

The Chief of Staff said one other thing of interest:

'The new team members don't fly with anyone in the back seat 'til they get to SPRINGHAWK. (That is) the cut off'.

Flight Lieutenant Stark was a new member. Exercise SPRINGHAWK, the 5-week pre-season training deployment to Greece, commenced a month *after* the accident. (The aim being to gain Public Display Approval from Air Officer Commanding. Once awarded, the pilots are allowed to wear their red flying suits, groundcrew their blue coveralls).

Setting aside for a moment that Jon had not completed his training, the implication is that he should have flown with a different pilot. The Panel did not discuss this contradiction.

*

I have avoided discussing Flight Lieutenant Stark's evidence to the Panel. Much of it was redacted, yet in court the President read out the redactions at the Coroner's request. (The family had been provided with an unredacted Part 1 of the Service Inquiry report). I will respect the redaction, but there was nothing untoward and certainly nothing more than any other pilot would say. Throughout the witness evidence there was universal praise for his abilities; especially from the Chief of Staff, whom he had instructed some years before.

General

'Service Inquiry' is a misnomer. It is a limited investigation. MoD argues

that it is not a criminal court of law, so the principles inher
criminal justice system do not apply; and indeed it is not constrainᴇᴜ ᴜ,
the normal rules that everyone else must abide by. That is to say, it can
do as much, or as little, as it pleases. So if not intended to form part of
the judicial system, what purpose does it serve?

The Armed Forces Act and the Armed Forces (Service Inquiries)
Regulations set out the requirement to investigate. But the Inquiry does
not conform to any recognised format, primarily because it is not
independent. It is tasked to consider human factors, but expressly
forbidden to consider or apportion blame. But that merely hides from
public view that secondary investigations *will* take place, and
subordinates *will* be blamed; often to protect the guilty.

A good example of this occurred after the aforementioned RN Sea King
mid-air, an investigation taking place into the Board of Inquiry's main
Contributory (and arguably Causal) Factor. It ceased immediately when
the 'accused' produced evidence showing a superior was culpable. In the
face of his written report to the investigator, the RN continues to deny
the investigation took place.[20]

Service personnel decide what evidence is relevant, and no opportunity
to protect the interests of the deceased is afforded. The entire
investigation is conducted in private. It is a one-way street, with families
not permitted to ask questions or even be represented. The Inquest,
often some years later, is their first and only opportunity to have MoD
cross-examined; by which time MoD will have posted those who could
answer questions. And it is MoD's position that once a person, military
or civilian, is posted, there is no obligation to respond.[21] Moreover, at
the Inquest in November 2021 MoD's QC, Edward Pleeth, argued that a
witness could only answer questions arising from his time in post. The
Coroner concurred, nullifying her Inquest.

Until the Panel reports, it is entirely the 'property' of the President. In
theory he can ignore any input or pressure from other sources,
regardless of status and rank. However, his subsequent career may be
subject to the recommendations of those he is reporting to. And these
senior officers are not bound to accept his findings. They may substitute
their own judgment without offering any justification. It is this finding

---

20 Letter report SPCISR2f-pf, 25 February 2004.
21 MoD letter D2PT xxxxxx, 15 February 2007. (Personal identifier redacted).

that is recorded as the final decision, against which there is no appeal.

There are many examples of interference by senior officers, confirmed by the late Mr William Tench, former head of the (then) Accidents Investigation Branch, and a distinguished fighter pilot during World War II. The Minister of State for Defence Procurement, Lord Trefgarne, had asked him to conduct a study of military aircraft accident investigation procedures. He reported in January 1987, but senior military commanders complained his recommendations would take away their absolute power. They succeeded in having the government suppress the report. When interviewed by the BBC in 2009 after the report was uncovered, Lord Trefgarne described his feelings as those of *'despair'*. He confirmed that the primary pressure came from the Chief of the Air Staff, Air Chief Marshal Sir David Craig; who, as Lord Craig, later supported the findings against the Chinook ZD576 pilots.

Mr Tench confirmed *'mediocre standards where investigations are conducted by complete novices'*. Harsh, but true. He cited accidents where the wrong causes were identified, and where investigators missed recurrences. His main criticism was:

'A disturbing feature is the influence senior officers seek to exert on the investigation process, particularly in the RAF. The pervasive nature of the involvement of some Station Commanders, senior Staff Officers, and even Commanders-in-Chief, is an unwelcome intrusion upon what should be the complete independence of the Board. The opportunities for Staff Officers to influence the Board's interpretation of evidence, or their findings, must throw doubt on the complete freedom of the Board to draw its own conclusions. It must, of course, always be possible to have reservations about the findings of an Inquiry, but to assume superior insight on a basis of rank must be more doubtful. It is my considered view that Boards of Inquiry have outlived their usefulness as instruments of efficient aircraft accident investigation'.

A month after he wrote this, on 27 February 1987 Chinook HC Mk1 ZA721 crashed in the Falkland Islands, killing all seven onboard. The President of the Board of Inquiry had the findings dictated to him. These were contrary to the physical evidence from the scene.[22]

Later, the Public Accounts Committee commented on the position of reviewing officers, recommending:

---

22 The Senior Inspector on Chinook ZA721, Mr Tony Cable, later led the Chinook ZD576 Mull of Kintyre, PanAm Lockerbie and Air France Concorde investigations.

'The process should be revised to ensure that those officers who control the findings of Boards of Inquiry should not be those who also have management and command responsibility for the aircraft and personnel involved'.

Put another way, and as noted by Mr Tench, a body which is the regulator, Convening Authority and final arbiter is unlikely to contribute much to air safety.

*

Political influence is always a factor, and there is a real conflict of interests. As with other aspects of management of the Armed Forces, the authority to convene an Inquiry is delegated from the Secretary of State for Defence. One might reasonably assume that the same level of ministerial accountability to Parliament would apply as with any other department. However, successive governments have rejected, for example, calls for an independent assessment of the issues that brought about the Nimrod and Mull of Kintyre Reviews. This refusal to act on known violations lies behind many deaths, including Jon's.

Article 6(1) of the European Convention on Human Right states:

'In the determination of his civil rights and obligations or of any criminal charge against him, everyone is entitled to a fair and public hearing within a reasonable time by an independent and impartial tribunal established by law'.

Despite the difficulties involved in identifying the precise role of a Service Inquiry, and especially the reviewing officers, its extra-judicial status does not preclude the application of Article 6. The European Court of Human Rights has ruled that the applicant's right to a fair hearing is violated if denied full participation in the hearing.[23][24] Yet MoD's denial of these rights extends beyond Service Inquiries to (e.g.) internal disciplinary hearings, where the inalienable right to representation is often denied, no evidence is required of the 'prosecution' (superiors), or allowed to be presented by the defendant.

Key evidence is routinely withheld, depriving the families the opportunity to have it impartially assessed. In the case of Sean Cunningham (Hawk XX177, 2011) it was discovered *after* the Inquest that the Military Aviation Authority had attended the meeting that approved the illegal servicing directive that led directly to his death. Also, that MoD was sitting on video evidence that proved RAF culpability. The

---

23 Feldbrugge v, The Netherlands. May 29, 1986 (No. 294B), 18 E.H.R.R. 425.
24 'The Juridicial Review' (Andrea Batey, 2001).

Inquest was not reopened, and despite being aware of who was responsible, and being shown the video evidence, the Health and Safety Executive prosecuted Martin-Baker.[25]

These violations may not be the norm, and may even be rare (MoD will not comment, except to support them), but it cannot be coincidence that the best known examples relate to staff who reported systemic failings in the Safety Management System. This persistent misconduct provided the motivation that ultimately led to the Nimrod Review.

---

25 'Red 5' (David Hill, 2019).

6. Cause of the accident

An Engine Failure After Take-Off (EFATO) is the most time and energy-critical emergency, requiring skilful handling and continuous situation assessment to ensure a safe outcome. Careful pre-take-off consideration and emergency take-off briefing of the available courses of action, in the prevailing conditions, is essential.

During a Practice EFATO the aim is not to land, but to complete a turn and conduct a go-around over the same runway, in the same direction as take-off. A 'touch and go' is not permitted because the aircraft is too heavy at the normal take-off weight. Pilots are warned that the minimum speeds advised in manuals merely ensure one is in the best position to meet the objective; which is to practice gliding within a stated speed range while buying time to make a decision as to what is possible, and when it would be safer to eject.

In the Hawk, an EFATO is defined as an engine failure at any point up to 300 knots. Above that a failure is not considered an EFATO and the pilot may position the aircraft for any suitable runway. A 'turnback' is defined as *'returning to the reciprocal runaway during the take-off phase if speed is below 300 knots'*. This is now prohibited in Red Arrows aircraft, following several accidents while practicing the exercise.[26]

The actions required in the latter stages of a PEFATO and turnback are the same; and the single term 'turnback' used to be common. Pilots are cautioned to maintain the correct speed and, if necessary, make an early decision to overshoot at not less than 300 feet Above Ground Level.

These manoeuvres are challenging, because the aircraft is low on potential and kinetic energy at take-off. Pilots should not expect to succeed every time. They are taught:

- If the engine fails between becoming airborne and selection of landing gear UP, the aircraft may be abandoned or, if only just airborne, an attempt made to land on the remaining runway. Sometimes the safer option is to get airborne and then make an approach and land.

- If the engine fails between the time the landing gear is selected UP

---

26 Red Arrows Display Directive, Part 3 paragraph 20, and Part 1 paragraph 64a, note 20.

and 250 knots (clean or with stores/pylons fitted), or 270 knots (aircraft with non-jettisonable wing stores), abandon the aircraft.

- If between 250/270 and 300 knots, commence a turnback.

Following an EFATO, stores must be jettisoned and one climbs and turns towards the selected runway. An emergency radio call is made, but the emphasis is on flying an accurate turn and maintaining speed. When certain of reaching the aiming point, flaps are lowered and a minimum speed is maintained. The main factors determining success are the ability to (a) make a prolonged turn whilst maintaining the minimum gliding speed and avoiding the onset of stall, and (b) land and stop the aircraft safely, even with the assistance of a barrier.

If the pilot is in any doubt as to the ability to recover safely, he is told *'not to delay the ejection decision'*. However, this does not cater for carrying an inexperienced passenger who, perhaps, may have to be talked and encouraged through what to do (notwithstanding any brief training he/she may have received).

PEFATO continuation training was mandated in other Hawk squadrons, but for the Red Arrows it was deemed sufficient to conduct a *'non-specific Practice Forced Landing'* every 90 days. (The overarching term under which PEFATO falls. Other types are Radar and Visual). This meant there was no easy way of knowing if a pilot had conducted a PEFATO. The Team Leader's argument was that it did not matter, as the *'core skill was the same'*. This may have merit, but the squadron was out of step with other RAF Hawk users, the Service Inquiry noting *they* conducted PEFATO training every 30 days. (As noted, Flight Lieutenant Stark averaged over two per month when at 100 Squadron). It was recommended that currency requirements for core handling exercises be reviewed across the Hawk fleets.

Configuration Control

This is what facilitates a pilot entering his aircraft, recognising it for what it is, and using it safely.

Why was the recommendation specific to Hawk T.1, when XX204 was a T.1A? The Aircrew Manual states:

'The Hawk T.1 is a flying training and weapons training aircraft. The Hawk T.1A is equipped to an operational standard capable of undertaking a war role; the equipment for this role is also suitable for the weapons training role'.

The Panel didn't actually ignore the T.1A, saying elsewhere:

'For the purpose of this report the difference between the Hawk T.1 and 1A are irrelevant and the aircraft will be referred to as a T.1 throughout'.

Complicating matters, the Panel did not refer to the T.1W. During the initial T.1 production run (late 1970s) it was decided that some aircraft would be in the pure flying training role, and a Service Designed Modification removed the weapons control boxes. If refitted, the aircraft became a T.1W; either because they could not be reverted to their original build standard, or could but the cost was excessive. It is unclear how many T.1Ws were created, but the figure would seem to be in the 20s. Between April 2000 and August 2003, 80 aircraft were rebuilt by replacing the centre and rear fuselages with standard Mk60 series components. (The uprated export version). These modifications extended the safe life of the structure, the previous 6,000 hours being extended to over 10,000 hours. The 80 comprised 11 T.1s, 62 T.1As, and 7 T.1Ws. That is, the three Marks operated concurrently.

*

Suspecting another anomaly in the audit trail, I sought the T.1/1A/1W Release(s) to Service under Freedom of Information. The RAF provided the T.1/T.1A version, stating:

'There is no Release to Service for the Hawk T.1W as the RAF does not operate this aircraft'.[27]

At time of writing the Red Arrows fly one T.1W, going so far as to welcome input from the public as their engineers *'would love to find out more about this model'.*[28]

When asked when the T.1W left Service, and to provide a copy of the last T.1W Release, or the last Release mentioning it, the RAF replied that the information was not held, adding:

'The Hawk T.1W is the former designation of the Hawk T.1A. We have been unable to identify when the designation of these aircraft changed'.[29]

Quite apart from the mandate to retain airworthiness records, the above cannot be reconciled; which is always a systemic failure. Also, Part G of the Release, 'RTS History', is blank, which is perhaps what the officer

27 Letter, Air Command Secretariat 2022/03343, 8 April 2022.
28 E-mail Red Arrows Public Relations Office, 14 February 2022 10:52.
29 Letter, Air Command Secretariat 2022/04688, 10 May 2022.

responding to the request looked at. It is at Issue 5, but does not record any changes pre-April 2021.

I conclude there was no Release for the T.1W and MoD was seeking a form of words to avoid admitting this.

*

If an MoD Technical Agency, the named individual responsible for maintaining the Build Standard, were permitted input to the report, he would take cognisance of the differences between T.1, T.1A and T.1W. He would not dismiss them as *'irrelevant'*. They are fundamental. Such an approach would get to the nub of the issue - the Build Standard had not been maintained. At a stroke, a valid line of inquiry was disregarded.

It was a retired Technical Agency whose evidence led to the Nimrod Review (which, arguably, reset aviation safety world-wide) and formation of the Military Aviation Authority (MAA). The MAA would consider him unsuitable for any job there. He, on the other hand, would think it a backward step professionally to be promoted into the MAA. And the MAA's Suitably Qualified and Experienced Person criteria falls far below that required of a Technical Agency. Resolve those incongruities and matters would improve overnight.

Stalling

A stall is an aerodynamic condition which occurs when smooth airflow over the aircraft's wings is disrupted, resulting in loss of lift. Specifically, when the Angle of Attack - the angle between the chord line of the wing and the relative wind - exceeds the wing's critical Angle of Attack.[30] This condition must be established through testing, for each aircraft type, in each approved configuration. This last is critical, because the Red Arrows configurations were not reflected in the Aircraft Document Set.

Stalls may be benign or violent. However, at times it may not be obvious that the aircraft *has* stalled. The condition can occur very quickly and is exacerbated if in the turn, as the outer wing will be going faster, is more efficient, and will be trying to roll the aircraft in the direction of the lower wing; accompanied by rapid loss of height.

In the basic (clean) configuration the T.1 and T.1A are aerodynamically

---

30 The chord line is an imaginary straight line joining the leading edge and trailing edge of the wing.

identical, with common stalling characteristics. The difference is the T.1A can carry external pylons and stores, including the smoke pod, and it is these that alter the flying and stalling characteristics.

Onset

In many aircraft a stall warning system may provide an audio tone, a light, or a device that vibrates one of the controls. In Hawk, the first indication and only reliable symptom of approaching stall is the onset of aerodynamic buffet, as speed and attitude symptoms are masked.

This is felt as a 'tapping' on the wings caused by breaker, or stall, strips - small components shaped like a Toblerone™ fixed to the leading edge of the wing to modify its aerodynamic characteristics. (Along with wing fences). They are designed to give marginally earlier pre-stall buffet, initiating air flow separation on a region of the upper surface of the wing during flight at high angle of attack. They also help to avoid a tendency to spin following a stall, and improve the controllability of the aircraft as it approaches the stall. As speed is decreased (Angle of Attack increased) buffet increases and some slight lateral unsteadiness develops which is controlled with ailerons.

Flight Lieutenant Stark reported that there was no pre-stall buffet at all. He was an experienced pilot, but how familiar was he with the stall warning and stall characteristics with a smoke pod fitted during a final turn in the configuration that he was flying? Were the procedures, such as minimum Indicated Airspeed and maximum bank angle, consistent with his previous training? Was there a maximum fuel weight with a full smoke pod when flying a PEFATO? What was the Red Arrows PEFATO profile with respect to energy (airspeeds and altitudes)? While the Panel touched on some of these issues, their work was made almost impossible by the poor Aircraft Document Set.

Stall

A stall is characterised by an uncontrolled roll, pitch or yaw motion (e.g. a wing drop, often with simultaneous nose down pitch), roll, pitch or yaw oscillations, increased buffet level, full back stick, or an uncontrollable descent rate.

If flown beyond the stall by moving the control column further aft, some yaw may develop which causes a tendency to roll. Ailerons alone may not be adequate to control the roll if the yaw is not checked, by use of rudder. As the speed lowers, and with the control column fully aft, the aircraft has an increased tendency to yaw and roll; it will descend at a high sink rate but with the airspeed increasing, and pitch oscillations may occur. This fully aft stick condition creates a different hazard - it may interfere with access to the Seat Pan Firing Handle.

This tendency to roll is doubly dangerous because it will take the aircraft outwith the ejection seat parameters, emphasising the need for an early decision to abandon the aircraft. That is, *in extremis* one could be ejected into the ground when the aircraft is inverted.

Stall Margin

Poor warning on finals is widely considered the worst characteristic of an aircraft that, overall, is benign and pleasant to handle. During the final turn, or on final approach, there is limited natural warning of the onset; so much so that if encountered a stall will occur. In an aircraft that has poor stall warning it is common to specify a maximum bank angle that may be used at the minimum speed. In Hawk, this should be no more than 45°.

To be effective, stall warning must be clear, timely and unmistakable. There must be enough margin between warning and the stall to allow for recovery. In level flight this is typically considered to be with respect to Indicated Airspeed (IAS), but in a turn it can be *either* a speed margin if at a constant bank angle, or g-force (or g-force margin, or load factor) in a constant IAS turn. It is in the Red Arrows configurations, and when stores are mounted, that uncertainty exists. The warning is less clear, and even less timely. Therefore, while buffet must be considered a warning, it should not be the only one.

The Aircrew Manual warns:

'The margin between buffet onset Indicated Airspeed (IAS) and the minimum IAS is typically 6 knots. A margin of less than 4 knots is unacceptable'.[31]

---

31 AP 101B-4401-15 Aircrew Manual, Supplement 2, paragraph 57 (Flight Test Schedule).

Yet, elsewhere it states that the margin is as low as 3 knots. That is, the pilot's primary reference admits the safety margin is unacceptable; and so by definition a flight safety critical hazard. Moreover, the Service Inquiry experienced a 2-4 knot margin during testing; hence its conclusion that the pilot had insufficient time to recognise the warning, decide his recovery action, and undertake it.

The margin also relies on the stall being defined by a fully aft stick, so the margin between buffet onset and the real aerodynamic stall, where lift starts to be lost, may be even less. And there exists the possibility of re-stalling if an aggressive pull into a climb is flown.

Mitigation is required in the form of layered defences. And in such a critical manoeuvre these defensive barriers must be high and strong. But the Assistant Chief of the Air Staff, by signing the Release to Service, stated that the risk was ALARP and Tolerable. So too other Duty Holders. Manifestly, these declarations were wrong. In fact, when taken with historical trends and deaths, the above goes a long way to satisfying the criteria for a Class A (highest level) risk. Again, that is unacceptable.

Stall recovery

If buffet is experienced on finals, and to minimise height loss, the pilot must carry out a Standard Stall Recovery. FTP3225H (the Hawk Training Manual):

'Unload to eliminate buffet, Select Full Power, Wings level - use aileron, Climb - as engine power "bites" select climbing attitude, raise landing gear and flap when positive rate of climb'.

But the Aircrew Manual, the definitive document, merely says:

'Recovery at any stage is immediate upon moving the control column forward'.

Once out of the stall, a climbing attitude is selected, taking care not to re-stall the wing. Of note, in the Hawk T.1 engine spool-up from idle is very slow, although Red Arrows aircraft have a different engine variant with slightly better acceleration. Only the lead position aircraft is permitted to fly in displays without a modified engine; and Reds 2 and 3 may do so during training provided no aircraft are flying outside or directly behind them. As Flight Lieutenant Stark was Red 3 it was important to state, for the record, what engine variant he was using.

Configuration Buffet

While not relevant here, this is caused by lowering of the landing gear, flap settings, or deploying the airbrake (on the underside of the rear fuselage), and is felt as a 'rumbling' underneath the aircraft. (During a display, deploying the airbrake will make the smoke colours deeper, as the engine will be running hotter). This should not be confused with the aerodynamic buffeting discussed above.

With the flaps selected to FULL there is some configuration buffet generated. This increases noticeably when the aerodynamic buffet that constitutes stall warning occurs, tending to undermine the requirement that stall warning be unmistakeable. With the smoke pod fitted the buffet is very different, the aircraft being more stable laterally.

General

While here is not the place to delve into the detailed history of Hawk aerodynamic design, suffice to say that in 1974 MoD jointly funded a detailed study of the aircraft's stall characteristics, and this work continued for many years. A particular concern was tailplane stalling causing what was termed the 'Phantom Dive'. Its positioning left much to be desired and much work went into amelioration, with many iterations of Tailplane Canard Vanes developed; especially for the US variant which had to be able to land on carrier decks.

Taking this long history of stall investigations and redesign into account, one cannot help but conclude that the characteristics experienced by Flight Lieutenant Stark were not unknown, but corporate memory within MoD had been lost.

If the reader wishes to explore this area further, may I recommend 'The Hawk Story', by Harry Fraser-Mitchell, Head of Hawk Aerodynamics (1971-81).

The Forced Landing Contract

An Actual or Practice Forced Landing should only be continued below 300 feet Above Ground Level if all the following criteria have been met:

- Landing gear is locked DOWN.
- Clearance to touch and go (Practice Forced Landing) has been received from Air Traffic Control.

- DOWN flap is indicated, or has been selected and is traveling.
- Heading is within 30° of runway heading.
- Angle of bank is less than 45°.
- Speed is between 150 and 170 knots.

This is the Forced Landing Contract. During a PEFATO one is practicing the ability to meet the Contract at 300 feet. If it is evident that all the criteria will not be achieved by 300 feet, a swift decision to go-around or eject must be made. The Contract is thus central to the pilot's decision-making; and it is important not to confuse an exercise where one's pride and perceived ability is at stake, with a learning exercise. The decision to go-around can be made by the pilot or directed by Air Traffic Control. Its execution is described in FTP3225H:

'Select full power and hold a steady attitude until the power bites, before setting the normal 8° nose up climb attitude'.

The Aircrew Manual offers no such instruction. In practice, if not flown from a wings-level attitude with low rates of descent, a go-around is normally flown using a blended roll to wings-level and pitch, to arrest the descent and achieve a climb away from the ground, as full power is simultaneously applied. This was the technique intended by Flight Lieutenant Stark. Did he achieve the Contract? The Panel settled on:

'Given XX204's position and flight parameters at the end of the downwind leg, it was extremely unlikely it could successfully achieve the Contract and runway centreline. The Panel concluded that the height and lateral spacing at the end of the downwind leg were intrinsically linked and therefore the position from which XX204 commenced the final turn, at 180 knots, was a Contributory Factor. Analysis of XX204's final turn was conducted in the Hawk Synthetic Training Facility. Several techniques were flown and while landings were achieved on a few occasions, at no time were all the Contract parameters met'.

That is not definite proof, so the question remains open. The Panel being prevented from discussing blame would necessarily restrict its comments, and it is possible much has been left unsaid. But it is already evident that the Aircraft Document Set did not reflect the aircraft flown. This is the worst kind of failure, because a series of formal declarations were made that it did.

*

The Aircrew Manual warns:

'If speed falls below 170/175 knots when gliding flapless with landing gear

down, the high rate of descent and limited margin above pre-stall buffet make it doubtful whether a successful roundout can be completed'.

(The 'roundout', or flare, is a slow, smooth transition from a normal approach attitude to a landing attitude, gradually rounding out the flightpath to one that is parallel with, and just above, the runway).

Also, that during a glide approach:

'Maintain a minimum speed of 150 knots until the landing flare'.

Many pilots consider *'150 knots'* ambiguous. Some interpret it as applying once wings level and lined up with the runway. Others, that it is the minimum speed in the turn onto the runway heading.

As a non-pilot, and with an open mind, I read two versions of the Aircrew Manual - one from 1992 and one from 2018. My interpretation of the old manual was *wings level and lined up with the runway*. However, I found the newer version less clear, as this has been added at some point: *'Should a tighter than normal turn be required, speed must be increased above 165/170 knots'*. When considering the speed profile flown, it is possible this may have been significant in this accident. Either way, the Panel considered this inadequate, recommending:

'AOC 22 Group should commission testing to provide guidance on the relationship between speed and Angle of Bank in all glide configurations in order to minimise the risk of stall during low speed manoeuvring'.

References to the Contract and go-around procedure were added to the Aircrew Manual in March 2020, two years after the accident. Hitherto, both were only mentioned in FTP3225H.

Flying Training Publication 3225H

The Release to Service (the Master Airworthiness Reference) sets out the conditions under which Service regulated flying may be conducted. It sits at the head of the Aircraft Document Set and must list what aircraft (not equipment or training) publications are authorised. The Panel reported that publications *'lacked clarity and were open to interpretation'*. Therefore, any judgment of suspected error can only be made once these prior failures are examined and their effect understood.

There are three principal Air Publications associated with the Release:

- Aircrew Manual (Air Publication Topic 15) contains the detailed instructions to aircrew on how to fly the aircraft. Expanding on the

Release, it includes more detailed data on aircraft and systems limitations, handling information and systems warnings.

- Flight Reference Cards (Air Publication Topic 14) consists of the detailed checklists for essential operations to be undertaken by each member of the aircrew during the various phases of flight. They are a summary of the instructions contained in the Aircrew Manual, and so the two must <u>always</u> be aligned.

- Operating Data Manual (Air Publication Topic 16) contains extensive and detailed operating data outside the scope of the Aircrew Manual, covering the performance of the aircraft; for example, take-off and landing field length graphs, and fuel consumption figures. Its latest amendment state <u>must</u> be listed in the Release (but is not).

But of immediate concern to the cause of the accident was the new 1400 feet guidance, against the achieved ~1030 feet. It was based on a 'clean' aircraft configuration, whereas the aircraft's drag index is different with the 370kg smoke pod fitted. (And the weight of the pod was not recorded in the aircraft documentation). That is, FTP3225H did not reflect the Red Arrows Build Standard or Use.

The Panel concluded that the aircraft being ~370 feet lower than the new guidance was a Contributory Factor. However, the President later told the Inquest that had the pilot been aware of this 1400 feet guidance *'we wouldn't be sitting here today'*. That is, he now considered it a Causal Factor. His report has not been retrospectively updated.

*

Flight Lieutenant Stark's position was that there was *'inadequate guidance promulgated to Red Arrows pilots'* as 1400 feet was only mentioned in FTP3225H *'which was not a mandated Red Arrows reference document, and of which (he) was not aware'.*[32] He was referring to the fact that, unlike (e.g.) the Aircrew Manual, Red Arrows pilots did not have to sign to say they'd read it. When interviewed on 6 April 2018 he confirmed that he used *'3225's guidance'*; so the issue was not that he was unaware of FTP3225H, only that he had not been advised of the recent amendment.

However, it was omitted that the Red Arrows Display Directive, which he *did* sign for, stated that it should be read *'in addition to the relevant chapters of FTP3225H and Part 2 of the Aircrew Manual'.*[33] One could

---

32 Submissions on behalf of Flight Lieutenant David Stark, 20 April 2020.
33 Red Arrows Display Directive, Appendix 1 to Annex A.

reasonably argue that makes it mandated. However, and for example, in the Chinook ZD576 case (Mull of Kintyre, 1994) the Air Staff disagreed. There, Controller Aircraft's *statement* that the aircraft was not to be flown <u>had</u> to be read *in conjunction with* Boscombe's reports setting out the detailed reasons. The Air Staff's position was this *mandate* could be ignored.

This was the only reference to FTP3225H in the Directive. When asked at the Inquest, a Qualified Flying Instructor from the squadron correctly stated that the Aircrew Manual was the *'core document'*; which emphasised that pilots were having to rely on a lower order publication, with no guarantee that <u>any</u> publication was correct.

Stark confirmed that the Aircrew and Operating Data Manuals were grossly out-of-date, and out of step with each other. That, both omitted crucial handling specifics in the Red Arrows configuration. Also, both lagged behind FTP3225H. For example, none had evolved with the aircraft weight, which was now over 400kg heavier, primarily because they did not take account of the smoke pod; resulting in the maximum take-off weight being shown as 5300kg instead of 5700kg. (To put this in context, such is the effect of extra weight that special precautions have to be taken to ensure the squadron's 37kg wheel jack pannier is always carried by the aircraft with the lightest pilot).

While this particular error was corrected post-accident, it went unsaid that the Service Inquiry had been advised by the Central Flying School Agent at RAF Leeming that FTP3225H was *'in song with the Release to Service, Aircrew Manual and Flight Reference Cards'.*[34] Other evidence wholly contradicted this, the Panel noting as an 'Other Factor' that there was *'incorrect information contained within the Aircrew Manual'.* Importantly, and in defence of the School's Commandant, the Delivery Duty Holder, he would rely on *his* Agents when assuring himself the Aircraft Document Set could be reconciled. That is not to criticise the Agent. If one wants to know the status of publications, ask the Publication Authority, as he/they will know why they are not *'in song'.*

The management of Air Publications is a centralised airworthiness activity. By definition, then, these were systemic failings. But MoD denied *any* systemic failings. When asked about these matters at the Inquest, the Service Inquiry President was unable to answer, saying his

---

34 E-mail 100 Squadron Hawk T.1 Central Flying School Agent to Service Inquiry, 10 September 2018 18:03; forwarded at 18:04 to the Service Inquiry President.

technical specialists did not report them. The implication being none of the Panel could recognise the deficiencies, even after witnesses pointed them out. It was also omitted that the Officer Commanding Defence Aircrew Publications Squadron had reported:

> 'We do not have a <u>corporate memory</u> of the Hawk aircrew publications other than what we can physically find in our archives'.[35]

The retention of corporate memory is an essential component of airworthiness. Omitting this served to mask systemic failings.

The role of the Defence Aircrew Publications Squadron (formerly the RAF Handling Squadron) is crucial. It must be provided with advance notification of proposed hardware or software changes. Within the Services, it has sole responsibility for deciding whether a modification has an effect on the management of a system or handling of an aircraft. It has significant input to the Release to Service and hence the Safety Cases, being responsible for representing the as-flown configuration therein, and for the accuracy and suitability of the information.[36] It must approve any Flight Test Schedule, and acts as Acceptance Authority for the Aircrew Manual, Flight Reference Cards and Operating Data Manual. But not, it would appear, FTP3225H.

*

The Red Arrows cannot escape criticism; although on a relatively minor point compared to the serious failures above them. Invited to comment on the changes that resulted in the January 2018 issue of FTP3225H, they did not. This might help explain why the Panel came across examples of them not being supported through normal MoD channels. This is common with units that are somehow 'different' and permitted or required to deviate from the norm. (Pathfinder Platoon of 16 Air Assault Brigade is an example in the Army). They can never assume that materiel and financial provision has been made to cater for their different needs, and can soon find themselves shut out of the 'system'; if for no other reason than the formal process does not allow for alternatives. This can be as simple as a form used to tabulate required resources not having a 'Red Arrows' box to tick because the original assumption that all Hawk usage is the same has never been changed.

---

35 E-mail OC Defence Aircrew Publications Squadron to Service Inquiry Panel Aircrew member, 5 February 2019 09:49.

36 Defence Standard 05-123 and Joint Service Publication 553.

HQ Provisioning Authorities (civilian engineers, and more accurately troubleshooters) responsible for identifying and correcting such anomalies were disbanded in 1988, without replacement. They may not always have succeeded, but at least there was a postholder who could explain why; and whose job it was to be forthright with his 2-Star as to impact, and attend Screening Meetings to argue for, or protect, funding. (And, incidentally, were usually recruited as Technical Agencies on promotion). Today, front-line have no-one like this to turn to.

Regardless, it was incumbent upon the Publication Authorities to ensure the various publications could be reconciled. Plainly they did not, although the FTP3225H sponsor, correctly, sought comment from squadrons. Each has a focal point for ensuring aircrew are informed of such changes, but this one introduced time and resource risks so should not have been circulated until after AOC 22 Group's input. If not the AOC himself, then his Group Safety Officer or the Delivery Duty Holder. What did he/they say? We don't know, so yet again a key aspect of the investigation is contaminated by an apparent desire to avoid drawing the Operating Duty Holder into court.

The Red Arrows are so badly under-resourced, did they think *What's the point?* (Perhaps the kitchen was untidy or the sandwiches curly, and took priority?) The decision to deny them an Air Safety Management Team, compounded by the short-handed Central Flying School team and a significant shortfall in engineers, was demoralising and ruinous. But whatever the reason, and whatever the procedure, a positive statement one way or the other was required; not least because nil reply is usually taken as consent.

On the final day of the Inquest the Delivery Duty Holder quite clearly pointed the finger at a previous witness, the aforementioned Qualified Flying Instructor, as being responsible for the information not reaching Flight Lieutenant Stark. This was not put to the witness so he was unable to defend himself, and no Publication Authority was called. Again, this diverted attention away from the systemic breaches.

*

The Panel and Inquest dwelt on FTP3225H, but the real issue is that the Aircraft Document Set was invalid - repeating a root cause of Sean Cunningham's death in 2011. When joining a squadron, pilots must sign to say they have read and understand (e.g.) the Flying Order Book, Aircrew Manual and Release to Service. As a result of this accident, beginning with the 2022 season they must also sign for FTP3225H. That implies all have been revalidated, reverified and reconciled. That is a lot of work, and it is not actually clear it has been done. The danger is that the FTP will continue to be regarded as a replacement for the Aircrew Manual. A solution emerges, requiring mandates to be implemented...

Training and the Hawk Simulator

Training is a risk control measure. It must have established aims, objectives, an associated syllabus, and be conducted by suitably qualified and experienced instructors using equipment (e.g. simulators) reflecting the in-use Build Standard(s) of the aircraft. The number of hours a pilot has flown does not equate to the quality of their decisions. One can have a thousand hours experience, or experience the same hour a thousand times. Expertise comes with experiencing and dealing successfully with a given situation. Ultimately, training must ensure common understanding of the requirement and sortie conduct, and that risks are identified and properly managed.

Pilots are placed under numerous constraints and requirements, and must maintain their currency. Opportunities to conduct a manoeuvre such as a PEFATO are rare, and to ignore one would leave the pilot open to criticism. But it was established that no common training objectives existed across the Hawk fleets, the Panel confirming that failure to conduct adequate pilot training was a major factor in the accident.

Moreover, Air Officer Commanding 22 Group stated in his interview with the Panel that the decision to *'detune'* the Red Arrows (i.e. reduce flying hours) was entirely funding-related. He also noted that their aircraft availability rate was extraordinary compared to other fleets, especially on an ageing aircraft type. However, one must be careful here, as the XX177 accident (Sean Cunningham, 2011) revealed dangerous shortcuts had been imposed on Hawk maintainers. One, *in situ* servicing of ejection seats, had been a root cause of Sean's death.[37]

Once in the aircraft, Jon's lack of training had no bearing on events. To prevent his own death he was required to acknowledge the order *'Eject, Eject. Eject'*, and pull his Seat Pan Firing Handle. The pilot managed one *'Eject'* before pulling his own Handle, a split second before impact. The RAF required the aircraft design to be such that he could not eject both seats. This decision, reaffirmed many times over decades, is crucial

---

37 'Red 5' (David Hill, 2019).

when assessing the cause of death, and is discussed in the next chapter.

*

The Hawk simulator is single-seat, dated, and does not replicate the feel of the aircraft. Nor does it cater for buffet, the smoke pod and its additional weight, or the different handling characteristics. Its ability to simulate an engine failure is limited to bird-strikes. It was not discussed whether the simulator, in which the pilot had just conducted a full engine shut down, could have given any false cues or perceptions. Much is missing in such a controlled environment, and here he went from feeling comfortable, to not right, in an instant. Instinctively he ejected. If *he* had no warning and no thinking time, what chance did Jon have?

At the Inquest, the RAF admitted that rather than modify the simulator it chose to carry the risk of performing live PEFATOs without being able to train adequately for them. Yet, in the same breath the witness claimed the simulator *'provided adequate training in all aspects'*.[38] He further declared that the Red Arrows imminent move to RAF Waddington, taking the simulator with them, would enable it to be suitably upgraded. If this can be done at Waddington, why not Valley? And if he believes it *'adequate'*, why upgrade at all? I'm playing Devil's advocate, asking the questions required of the scrutineer. A case must be made that the current simulator is <u>inadequate</u>. As matters stand an upgrade, or even an update, cannot pass scrutiny.

*

Duty Holders face a dilemma because servicemen must train realistically for war. A simulator must, as far as possible, accurately imitate what the aircraft does. Part of 'Requirements setting', in reality this is often an afterthought. Disconnects between aircraft and simulator Build Standards are common. There are rules designed to prevent this, one being that the simulator is regarded as the third aircraft, after the Trials and Proof Installation aircraft; ensuring, for example, it gets early delivery of avionics to minimise the lag between it and the aircraft.

The demise of the aforementioned HQ Provisioning Authorities, who managed this, meant training became regarded as part of logistic support, not the main development and production programme. Today it often lags by years, and is always vulnerable to cuts if there is an overspend elsewhere. (These Provisioning Authorities added the fine

---

38 Evidence of Group Captain Mark Jackson, 4 November 2021.

detail to what is generally a broad-brush Requirement from Main Building. They quantified every aspect of the Requirement; and if one does not quantify, one cannot cost the programme accurately. This is a constant source of frustration to MoD's procurers).

This failure is not confined to Hawk, or the RAF. In 1987 it was decreed (by an exchange officer) that the Sea Harrier FRS2 Operational Radar Trainer would not have Blue Vixen, the new radar. Instead, it was to retain Blue Fox from FRS1, which would be unsupportable. New pilots would turn up at their squadron, climb in, and say *'What's this?'*. The facility was dubbed the Sea Harrier Intensive Trainer.

The Apache AH-64D programme was another good example, the simulator contracted under the Private Finance Initiative (PFI) and delivered years late despite the programmatic risk being notified immediately (in 1996). In isolation bad enough, and parliamentary committees were scathing. But they were not told a concurrent RN programme in the same Directorate, faced with the same directive to delay its In Service Date by PFI-ing its Mission Trainer, refused, followed the regulations, and delivered ahead of schedule, under cost, and to a better specification.

I mention this to emphasise that training failures identified by the Service Inquiry were not the fault of the trainers.

Summary

The Service Inquiry President said the Panel members had asked themselves how a *'perfectly serviceable aircraft flown by an experienced pilot had stalled'*. He omitted that the Hawk T.1 fleet had no proper airworthiness certification. Lacking that, there can be no serviceability audit trail. That the Red Arrows engineers declared serviceability was due to them being told the certification, and hence the publications they worked to, were valid. In fact, they were deeply flawed. The regulations are clear. The Hawk should not have been flying without a written acceptance of the risks associated with MoD being unable to demonstrate airworthiness. This precise issue has been at the root of many accidents. The list is long and the death toll alarming.

In 1992 the RAF Director of Flight Safety reported that Chinook engineers were having to work to Argentinian publications captured in 1982, relating to a different Mark of aircraft - because the RAF's were inadequate. On 8 July 2016, Yak-52 G-YAKB crashed at Boscombe Down killing RAF test pilot Flight Lieutenant Alex Parr. The Service Inquiry recommended: *'The Empire Test Pilot School should have access to aircrew publications in English'.* (They were in Russian). Scandalous, but no Service Inquiry has said *Not again!,* and the systemic breach - failure to maintain the Build Standard - persists today.

*

It was Flight Lieutenant Stark's case that the smoke pod changed the handling characteristics to an unsafe degree. The RAF rejected this, stating:

'The difference in gliding performance between an aircraft with no external stores and one with a smoke pod is insignificant'.[39]

Hawk pilots I have spoken to agree with Stark; raising the question how much actual testing was done when the pod was cleared, and how much 'read across' was claimed from (e.g.) the similar gun pod. In turn, one would need to know how much testing of the gun pod took place. In other words, the full audit trail must be examined.

It is important to understand this background, because unverified read across is a well-known area of MoD violations. It is common to take dangerous short-cuts despite any or all of form, fit, function and use being different. This was a root cause in, for example, the aforementioned Tornado/PATRIOT shootdown and Sea King ASaC Mk7 mid-air, killing nine aircrew.

Given the sheer scale and scope of prior violations, and the need to subsequently amend the procedures (height, speed) and publications, I conclude that Flight Lieutenant Stark was badly let down by the RAF and MoD. I strongly suspect that many pilots will be thinking *There, but for the grace of God...*

Those responsible have yet to be interviewed.

---

39 Annex A to the statement of Group Captain Mark Jackson, 23 June 2021.

7. Points of divergence and cause of death

1. Supernumerary Crew - Why was Jon in the aircraft?

The general concept of Supernumerary Crew was conceived to enable experienced aircrew to fly in aircraft they were not qualified on. Over time, this has expanded to include certified groundcrew, and the rationale for them to deliver engineering support away from home base is set out in Regulatory Article (RA) 2340:

> 'On occasion, personnel other than a military registered Air System's Aircrew are required to be employed or carried where there is a justifiable and valid requirement; the scope of activity varies dependent on the Air System type and the task that is being conducted. Such personnel are not necessarily trained to the same level as Aircrew, nor do they undergo the same medical screening and as such there may be additional Risk to Life associated with the activity'.

An 'Air System' is the aircraft, piloted or remotely piloted, together with the ground-based systems vital to its safe operation. 'Aircraft' and 'Air System' are often conflated. The distinction is important when constructing Safety Cases, because these are tied directly to a stated form, fit, function and use.

When interviewed by the Panel, witnesses offered other reasons such as it was a *'morale tool'*. I agree with this, so long as any associated risk is tolerable and ALARP. But it was also said they provided an *'extra pair of eyes when flying a 9-ship'* and acted as a *'look-out'*. If a look-out is required, or desirable, what is the mitigation when none is available? (The concept is not unique. For example, some single-pilot helicopters require rear crew to move forward to act as look-out at certain points of the sortie; usually take-off and landing. But the rationale, and why they are not two-pilot aircraft, is always explained).

*

The fundamental difference between a passenger and Supernumerary Crew is the training required, and is set out in RA 2340:

> 'The Supernumerary Crew Certificate of Competence will provide auditable evidence that the individual has achieved the level of competency required by Aviation Duty Holder and Accountable Managers (Military Flying) orders to operate/be employed on the Air System'.

67

As Red 3's engineer, Jon was responsible for carrying out after/before flight tasks at RAF Valley, such as fuel/oil/oxygen replenishment. MoD's view on this, put by Group Captain John Monahan, at the time Commandant Central Flying School at RAF Cranwell, was that to be Supernumerary Crew it was sufficient that he *'contribute to the outcome of the overall mission'*. That, with experience, Circus engineers *'become part of the Red Arrows crew'*.[40] The Service Inquiry President countered by pointing out Jon and his colleagues contributed *'only when they got there and they're on the ground'*, so there was no imperative to fly there.

The Red Arrows Display Directive states that before flying as Circus <u>or</u> Supernumerary Crew, a training syllabus has to be completed. This concludes with (a) a simulator sortie, then (b) a <u>familiarisation</u> sortie. The *'or'* refers to occasions, such as during the first part of a display, when Circus, if onboard, fly as passengers - but by definition they must be certified as Supernumerary Crew to be in that position.

Only then can they train to fly in a Post Maintenance Test Flight, which includes a <u>shakedown</u> sortie. With the notable exception of the Officer Commanding, witnesses and the Service Inquiry Panel itself conflated 'familiarisation' and 'shakedown'. So too the Convening Authority, Director General Defence Safety Authority. The difference is that a Post Maintenance Test Flight includes limited aerobatics and exposure to higher and lower g.[41] When authorised, the specific aim of a shakedown flight must always be stated, such as 'air test'.

But Jon was undertaking his <u>familiarisation</u> sortie *before* simulator training. It must be said that the rules are overly complex, contradictory, and counter intuitive; and no two witnesses explained Supernumerary Crew in the same way. That being so, the rules are not fit for purpose and must be clarified. Also, as we shall see, a rule is useless if there is no means if complying with it.

*

RA2340 stated:

'Supernumerary Crew are not classified as passengers. A supernumerary crewmember is an individual, military or civilian, who is temporarily attached to an air system crew for the purpose of carrying out a specific duty not involved

---

40 Service Inquiry interview with Group Captain (now Air Commodore) John Monahan, 12-13 June 2018.
41 Red Arrows Display Directive, Part 1, Appendices 2 & 3 to Annex D.

with flying/operating the air system, as authorized by the appropriate Aviation Duty Holder or Accountable Managers (Military Flying)'.

Post-accident, this was changed to:

'A Supernumerary Crewmember is an individual, military or civilian, who is employed on an Air System and authorized to carry out a specific duty (that does not require an Aircrew qualification) while in flight or ground taxiing. This specific duty is to have an active role in achieving the purpose of the authorized flight and may involve the operation of Air System equipment/systems or authorized Equipment Not Basic to the Air System under the supervision of the Air System's Aircrew'.

The major difference is in *'operation of Air System equipment/systems or authorized Equipment...'.* This refers to the new rule whereby Circus are 'Tactical Passengers'. Only photographers, operating *'Equipment not Basic...'* such as cameras, and groundcrew taking part in a Post Maintenance Test Flight, are Supernumerary Crew.[42]

*

The mandatory simulator training had not been conducted in over 20 months. It had been booked for the previous month, but cancelled. Group Captain Monahan told the Panel:

'I found out two days after the crash, so I am now aware that I was not aware at the time and that's something I just simply wouldn't have condoned. So I was mightily annoyed about that when I found out'.

But he went on to say Jon was *'compliant because (Circus) doesn't have to complete (simulator training) until the beginning of the display season, based on the fact we're looking at the risk of bird-strike'.*

The problem is, birds tend not to avoid Red Arrows aircraft just because their display season has not yet commenced. Monahan conceded that there had been no risk assessment of Circus not having done simulator training; and any training was not formally recorded.

However, the strongest evidence was provided by Circus Team Leader Chief Technician William Allen (a Sergeant at the time), who had flown in the rear seat of one of the other Hawks. Asked at the Inquest *'What did you understand your status to be?'*, he replied:

'Passengers. The report says we were Supernumerary Crew, but we were

---

42 Red Arrows Display Directive Part 1, Appendix 1 to Annex D.

passengers'.

It was he who selected the three Circus members to undertake the trip. His attempts to organise their simulator training had been rejected, so he knew that, by definition, they were only passengers. He knew they were allowed to undertake the flight, but not permitted in the aircraft when a PEFATO was attempted. He did not know that Jon's pilot intended to perform the manoeuvre.

*

In November 2021, and having heard Allen's sworn testimony, the Coroner asked the Service Inquiry President:

'Did the Panel consider the confusion or have difficulty in establishing status?'.

He replied that the Panel had *'assumed'* training had been completed. Yet when interviewed on 15 May 2018 Allen had firmly stated, under oath, they had <u>not</u> carried out their simulator training, emphasising that *he* had <u>never</u> flown as Supernumerary Crew. He confirmed the training had been cancelled *'due to lack of manpower'*; both aircrew and engineers. There was no confusion in his mind, and nor should there have been in the Panel's - and Allen's assertion was easily fact-checked. Furthermore, there was no evidence of <u>any</u> Circus members being authorised as Supernumerary Crew.

The President was not asked why he disregarded Chief Technician Allen's evidence. Instead, he relied on telephone discussions the previous evening between the Officer Commanding Red Arrows (Red 11), the Team Leader (Red 1), and Group Captain Monahan, during which the latter verbally endorsed them as Supernumerary Crew. This was then noted in his Air Safety Decision Register, but the three Circus engineers were not informed of it.

Nor was the squadron's Safety Officer; who later gave evidence that Circus status for those sorties on Tuesday 20 March had been identified as an issue at the end of the previous week, and he had discussed this with Reds 1 and 11. Asked if Circus had flown as Supernumerary Crew the previous year without training, he replied *'Yes'*.

The Junior Engineering Officer (Circus 1) confirmed this extended back to at least Autumn 2016, when she joined. She elaborated on the reasons - there was an extensive ongoing modification programme; a lengthy period of particularly poor aircraft serviceability when they were down to 10; and she was short of at least 11 engineers so none could be released even if the training was available. The mitigation was that the (previous)

Team Supervisor (Red 10) would give them an extensive verbal briefing. This had been planned again, but the new Red 10 was unavailable.

She also confirmed that, at the same point in *her* training (conducting her familiarisation flight), she was a passenger, not Supernumerary Crew.[43]

*

The above was contradicted by the Team Leader, Red 1. In his initial evidence to the Defence Accident Investigation Branch on 22 March 2018, he stated:

'They had all done their training, they had their qualifications'.

It would appear he double-checked, because on 9 April 2018, when interviewed by the Panel, he stated:

'(Jon's) status to me was Supernumerary Crew, but cognisant of the fact he had not met one of the criteria'.

And then:

'Yes, that was the conversation I had with the OC. I wanted to make sure that we are absolutely aware that they haven't done the simulator training, and there's a reason we made that call [to Monahan] *about the simulator training, and whether they were therefore then supernumerary crew'.*

But Monahan's evidence was that lack of simulator training and non-certification was not discussed. What, then, did he think he was signing for? Given that his decision was recorded in his Decision Register, one might have expected the Panel to quote it. It did not. I'm afraid this is a very serious discrepancy on one of the root causes of death. Either Monahan was told of the issue on the evening of 19 March, or he was not. This matter alone requires the Service Inquiry to be reconvened.

Another important issue arises out of this. The Panel ignored Chief Technician Allen in favour of his superiors at the squadron. And then ignored *them* in favour of Group Captain Monahan. Which brings us back to something mentioned earlier - MoD's policy that senior officers cannot be wrong by virtue of their rank.

The general quality of evidence was in inverse proportion to rank. Of all those involved, only one can be right. Plainly, that is Chief Technician Allen. But it is clear the Panel recognised the discrepancies.

---

43 Service Inquiry interview with Red Arrows Junior Engineering Officer, 15 May 2018.

It didn't spell them out, but left a trail of clues. This is common. Service Inquiries dare not tell the whole truth, but will leave hints that they know will be missed by (e.g.) the Defence Safety Authority when reviewing the report, but picked up later by the public. (Yes, I know… but my point is proven).

*

The Panel noted that the flight was deemed 'Continuation Training', covering *'all events in which Red Arrows pilots are required to maintain currency'*, and so the conduct of a PEFATO was *'implicit within the authorization'*. That is correct, so long as no passenger or Supernumerary Crew was in the rear; although the Team Leader opined that he would have liked to have known if a PEFATO was intended. Perhaps, then, the rules were inadequate?

Stark told the Panel that he intended to conduct a PEFATO at RAF Valley, and then an unspecified type of Practice Forced Landing upon his return to RAF Scampton. He advised RAF Valley Station Operations of his intent at 1250, shortly before departure. Jon was then briefed on the way out to the aircraft.

He also confirmed that he knew Circus had not carried out their simulator training. But also that he understood Group Captain Monahan had signed them off as Supernumerary; although he was not asked how or when this had been conveyed to him. That is, he (Stark) understood the rules, and thought Monahan had issued a waiver. This flight was to be the first time he had flown in the Red Arrows with a rear seater, and *'it was a conscious thought on my part that I'm okay to do a PEFATO'*; implying that, had he believed Jon a passenger, he would not have permitted him in the aircraft.[44]

For her part, the Coroner's probing was later excellent, and it was clear she preferred Allen's first-hand evidence over what was effectively hearsay (as the officers were not in court).

Overriding contradictions

Contradicting the notion that Supernumerary Crew could fly in a PEFATO, RA2340 stated:

'Passengers or Supernumerary Crew should not be exposed to potentially

---

44 Service Inquiry interview with Flight Lieutenant David Stark, 6 April 2018.

hazardous flight regimes'.

By any standards a PEFATO is such a regime. The rules changed (again) after the accident, and the Red Arrows are no longer allowed to conduct a PEFATO with either passengers or Supernumerary Crew.

*

The Service Inquiry noted a further inconsistency:

'The Red Arrows Display Directive prohibited the carriage of personnel other than crew (except for Circus) for Practice Forced Landings commencing below 1000 feet; this prohibition included current non-Red Arrows Hawk pilots if flown as a passenger. Consequently, and as with this accident, an individual on his second flight could be exposed to a complex manoeuvre, yet an experienced and qualified on type Hawk pilot could not'.

The Display Directive is subordinate to, and not mentioned in, the Release to Service (the Master Airworthiness Reference), Group Air Staff Orders, or Military Aviation Authority regulations. Yet at the Inquest the Service Inquiry President stated it was the *'primary document'*, sitting above (e.g.) the Aircrew Manual, Flight Reference Cards and Operating Data Manual, which *are* invoked by the Release to Service.

The Panel recommended that Officer Commanding the Red Arrows:

'Should generate a more detailed authorization matrix to enable clear understanding of flight details for non-core role sorties when carrying passengers/Supernumerary Crew (and) should clarify the status of personnel undergoing training for employment as Supernumerary Crew, give clear direction regarding the capacity and restrictions of their employment, and formalise the Supernumerary Crew status in an auditable process so as to ensure that associated risk is managed.'

Concluding:

'The lack of clarity of Supernumerary Crew status and auditable endorsement had the potential for misinterpretation of an individual's qualifications which could result in exposure to an undue level of risk'.

That this undue exposure to a known risk was a root cause of death was left unmentioned. The Panel also omitted that sufficient expertise and awareness of the rules existed with both Chief Technician Allen and Flight Lieutenant Stark. And, presumably, the Team Leader and the Officer Commanding, who thought it necessary to disturb Group Captain Monahan the previous evening because they obviously knew that Circus members should be classified as passengers.

In her remarks, Director General Defence Safety Authority, Air Marshal (now Dame, and retired) Sue Gray, said:

'This was a straight forward sortie for which the dual requirement to complete Continuation Training and deliver Circus familiarisation led to Corporal Bayliss being exposed to a flight profile that would not be reasonably expected in his primary role as Supernumerary Crew'.

While confirming Supernumerary Crew should not be carried during a PEFATO, she too ignored that the rules had been waived, and Chief Technician Allen was correct.

Summary

Plainly, there is much missing here. Notably, and perhaps indicating how they were being pulled in different directions, the Panel pointedly referred to Jon as a passenger at the time of his pre-flight briefing at RAF Scampton (which could be interpreted as a comment on the above decision-making process), and throughout carefully differentiated between passengers and Supernumerary Crew.

What would persuade these officers to overlook a risk to life and seek a waiver? It emerged the Red Arrows were short of over 23 staff. Travelling by road to RAF Valley would require Circus to be away for two days, not a half day; and weary upon return yet required to work on aircraft - itself a major risk. Flying them in Hawks circumvented the need for a significant infrastructure to ferry them in a passenger aircraft.

However, in his evidence to the Panel Air Officer Commanding 22 Group asserted that he was *'not unduly short of support'*. This disagreement between the Panel, AOC and the squadron hierarchy was not discussed.

Regarding Red Arrows Bow-Ties, the Service Inquiry said it:

'Could find no evidence of where the flying of Supernumerary Crew or Circus had been considered, and consequently there was no evidence of the Supernumerary Crew training syllabus having been used as a barrier within a threat line'.

(See Figure 2. The *'threat line'* is that drawn between *'threat'* and *'hazardous event'*. The *'control measures'*, or *'barriers'*, are usually termed 'defences in depth'. This constant changing of terminology is confusing, but the modern way to advancement).

The most obvious organisational error, therefore, was to authorise a PEFATO with Jon in the rear seat. If he knew, it is unlikely he objected.

He lived for these experiences. The days are gone when young apprentices had the opportunity to fly on maintenance check flights. This provided two benefits. It was the ultimate incentive to do their work properly, in turn placing an onus on MoD to train them properly. The danger arises when the latter is viewed as an unnecessary expense, preventing the former. That danger is now the norm.

I will leave the final word to the Chief of Staff to Commandant Central Flying School:

'It is difficult to justify why they're not passengers each time they fly'.

2. Command Eject - Why did Jon remain in the aircraft?

If the pilot is alone, he simply pulls his Seat Pan Firing Handle and ejects. Matters are different if there are two occupants. In some aircraft, only the front seat occupant can initiate both seats. In others, neither or both can. In the Hawk, if Command Eject is OFF then each occupant ejects separately when they pull their Firing Handle. If it is ON, only the rear seater can eject both. This reflects the principle that Hawk is a training aircraft, and so the decision to eject both crew is with the instructor who is assumed to always be in the rear.

Therefore, the Aircraft Assisted Escape System is not fit for purpose if the instructor is in the front, and when any passenger is carried.

*

Command Eject is part of the before-flight briefing. Pilots are always concerned that a novice in the rear might be overwhelmed, and that much of their normal capacity is lost once they are strapped in and the canopy closed. For this reason they are not given control of the front seat, and Command Eject is OFF. As part of his pre-flight checks, the pilot ensures the system is set correctly. As a double-check, during taxi the passenger is challenged to confirm that the Command Selector Valve in the rear cockpit is 'DOWN and OFF'. Once seated, the pilot has no direct control over the selection, and there is no indication to him of status. The Selector lever is lift-guarded at both settings, and a rotatable knurled knob locks it at the selected setting. Once set, it is impossible to accidentally move its position.

If the Selector is 'UP and ON', and the rear seater pulls his Firing Handle, *his* seat ejects first. The front seat is delayed by 0.35 seconds to allow the rear seat to clear the airframe; and the rocket packs are configured so that the front seat is propelled slightly to port, the rear to starboard.

Briefly, the front seat only receives the gas pulse from the Command Delay Breech Unit and cannot send gas to the rear. Likewise, the rear seat only sends a gas pulse and cannot receive one. Both seats therefore require modifications to incorporate front seat Command Eject, as does the aircraft.

The essential point here is that Martin-Baker are fully aware how to implement any Command Eject logic, in any of their seat installations. However, it is MoD's position that the company did not know until mid-late 2021, after a feasibility study was conducted. Similarly, at the trial of Martin-Baker in 2018 it was claimed the company did not know how their seats worked. At time of writing their products have saved 7,675 aircrew from certain death. I shall leave it to the reader to form an opinion as to who knows what about ejection seats.

The risk

The Red Arrows concept of use is completely different to that of other Hawk users, but their Build Standard and Air System Safety Case do not reflect this. We know from the Sean Cunningham case (2011) that neither was valid, and now know (in 2022) they still aren't. The Service Inquiry did not go there, although concluded:

'The engineer's lack of experience to independently initiate an ejection was an Aggravating Factor. The provision of a front seat Command Eject facility may have resulted in both crew surviving'.[45]

But omitted that the Aircrew Manual states:

'If the independent ejection sequence is operative [i.e. Command Eject OFF] *the rear seat occupant should eject first'.*[46]

That is, the pilot was required to issue a timely order for Jon to eject, and consciously wait for him to do so. Might I suggest the latter is not easy - the subconscious desire for self-preservation will tend to prevail.

A firm statement was needed from the Panel that, at the RAF's insistence, the Command Eject system was not fit for the purpose to which the aircraft was being put. Also needed was an acknowledgement that even an experienced pilot can fail to recognise the need to eject. I

---

45 XX204 Service Inquiry report, paragraphs 1.4.354 and 1.4.364.
46 AP 101B-4401-15, Chapter 9.7.

discuss this later when reviewing the loss of Flight Lieutenant Philip Martin, killed in the same way Jon was; undoubtedly why MoD omitted any mention of that accident. By that single act of concealment, the investigation and Coroner's Inquest were nullified.

*

A major consideration is that individual vertebrae can only withstand large compressive loads if applied at right angles to the plane of the intervertebral disc. To adopt this posture (in effect, sit up straight with one's head against the head restraint), occupants need a little warning to prepare themselves. If they are leaning forward or twisting round, and experience an unexpected ejection, severe injury can result.

Hence, one reason a pilot is required to call out over the Intercom *'Eject, Eject, Eject'*. This had been briefed to Jon, but the pilot managed only one *'Eject'* before pulling his Handle. The media reproduced graphic images of him parachuting to the ground, with a fireball close behind. If he continued with the command, it would be inaudible as the Intercom is immediately disconnected during the ejection sequence.

The Panel concluded that the pilot would not have got out had he completed the command; and, given the reaction time required, Jon would not have got out anyway. This misses the above points, and ignores the Forced Landing Contract. Also, and even with the late decision to eject, had front seat Command Eject been fitted Jon would have went first and probably survived. Knowing *he* would be delayed might concentrate a pilot's mind on making a timely decision.

This concept of use evolved over time: a classic example of a common failing, whereby the extant form, fit, function and use is *assumed* safe, and a series of minor modifications or changes in use are waved through on the grounds that everything will *remain* safe. The cumulative effect is detrimental. While my experience is primarily on helicopters, I have listened to Westland berate the Services many times because a proposed Service Designed Modification *'works, but isn't safe'*, or *'it's safe, but doesn't work'*, or *'it doesn't work and isn't safe'* - and the Services carry on regardless. This is why design liability is a major issue before any contract is let; and why the Panel should have included at least a potted history of the risk assessments (if any) at each change of use.

Recording and managing the risk

The Convening Authority, Air Marshal Sue Gray, said in her remarks:

'Defence may have to assess if the risks associated with carrying passengers in the rear cockpit of the Hawk T.1 are tolerable'.

But risks have to be Tolerable and ALARP. Was this a slip, or a notion that passengers' safety need not meet the standards applied to aircrew? An uncomfortable question, but consider this...

Hitherto, Command Eject was dealt with briefly in the Red Arrows Air Safety Register, under risk RED/OTHR-1/05 'Service passenger initiating ejection of crew'. This was raised on 2 May 2012, stating:

OTHR-1	Pax operates ejection seat during flight	Worst crdible outcome is pilot and pax ejected and suffer major injuries

Pilots always fly with cmd eject to off so only pax will be ejected. Worst credible outcome becomes major injuries to pax only

Figures 6a/6b: Extracts from Red Arrows Air Safety Register *(MoD)*

So, only a matter of months after Sean Cunningham was killed during an ejection, an assumption was made, and endorsed by the entire hierarchy, that all ejections are survivable and successful, and passengers are less important. A striking omission, given MoD's policy of sharing Risk Registers with stakeholder Design Authorities, is any comment by Martin-Baker; who may have had something to say. Nor does it address the concept of passenger incapacitation. This can only be construed as wilful manipulation to reduce the Class of Risk, to avoid the cost of mitigation. It is solid evidence of recklessness.

This was not an isolated error. For example, risk RED/SE/02, relating to pilot or passenger incorrectly strapping in and initiating an ejection, said the same - *'Worst credible outcome is major injuries to pilot'*. Once again, that was the cause of Sean Cunningham's ejection. (But not his death. He was killed by the RAF's refusal to service ejection seats in accordance with Martin-Baker's instructions).

However, it is entirely possible Martin-Baker *did* comment. MoD has been known to create multiple Risk Registers, each in turn removing ever more embarrassing MoD-owned risks; the version offered depending on who is conducting the audit or inspection. The prime example of this was the 2003 Sea King mid-air, where three Registers were created. Only the first, the programme manager's official one, recorded the risks that occurred and caused the accident. As I mentioned earlier, their mitigation had been planned and agreed, but the work cancelled - by the official who then had the sanitised 2nd and 3rd Registers created. I concede, however, that such fraud is not an offence in MoD.[47]

The Panel recognised the defective Register, characterising it as: *'More of a personal record rather than a formal decision Register'*. True, and utterly damning, but I would express this differently. It doesn't present evidence, it is a decoration. Window dressing, giving the appearance of robust management. Either way, the credibility of Duty Holders, and with it the entire construct, is damaged beyond repair.

Risk mitigation

The Panel recommended that Air Officer Commanding 22 Group:

'Assess the feasibility of the incorporation of a Command Eject capability into the Hawk T.1 that would allow aircraft commanders to initiate the ejection sequence for occupants from either cockpit seat'.

The real issue was avoided - *Why was the recommendation needed in the first place?* The mandated procedures are clear, and the Panel should have set out why they were not implemented. I can say from experience that, had my Admiral (same level as AOC 22 Group) received such a recommendation, he would stretch his legs and wander down to my office and quietly ask what had gone wrong. His main concern was always that it was a systemic failing. He knew the process was tried and tested, and wanted to know where it had broken down. And get it fixed.

Here, for example, because both equipment and aircraft modifications were required, the Service HQ Modifications Section would have contacted BAe Systems and Martin-Baker to ascertain what previous work had been done, and have them update quotes. They are granted this access via the Post Design Services (PDS) contract. Also, they would speak to the Aircraft Fleet Manager to assess the best embodiment strategy; which the Technical Agency is required to endorse. (Because he is required to approve the most appropriate and cost-effective production strategy for the modification sets, and modification kit

---

47 Chief of Defence Procurement letter CDP 117/6/7, 19 November 2001.

assembly). This way, two typical obstacles to approval of the subsequent modification are eliminated quickly.

In parallel, the Technical Agency would recognise the Build Standard and Design Authority Safety Case (his responsibility), and Concept of Use, In-Use Safety Case and Release to Service (the RAF's), could not be reconciled; and task the company to assess the reconciliation task. And, separately, submit a modification proposal. The contractual vehicle is again PDS, as one is seeking to maintain the Build Standard.

So important is this entire subject, a nominated employee at all Design Authorities is authorised to commence work immediately without seeking MoD approval. His formal title is the Post Design Services Officer (PDSO), and he is appointed by the Technical Agency. (The closest most government employees get to the ability to hire and fire, and indicative of just how crucial this is). This unique delegation exists for one reason - to facilitate immediate action when hazards or risks to life become apparent. The work starts immediately and without question, with payment guaranteed. This not a blank cheque. The delegation is merely sufficient to allow for the Technical Agency not being immediately available to approve the task.

One must try to understand why this did not happen in 2018, and why it will take at least seven years from accident to mitigation. One reason is straight-forward. The above posts no longer exist. This is a management failure - the inability to recognise that the work is not volume-related. It must be done regardless of how many modifications kits or sets must be embodied. Also, as the Hawk T.1 Out of Service Date is 2030 this will require a waiver as the timescale will start impinging on the remaining useful life rule. (The requirement to demonstrate five years useful life before expenditure is approved).

*

In summary, the two key questions relating to <u>cause of death</u> are:

1. *Was the inability of the pilot to eject his passenger a known risk?* (Yes, it was recorded in the Red Arrows Risk Register).

2. *Was it mitigated to ALARP?* (No, but a declaration made that it was).

If passengers are to continue flying in Hawks, the design must be changed to reflect a different concept of use; and the decision that injury and death of passengers, but not pilots, is tolerable must be rescinded.

This sounds simple, but I refer to my previous comments about Requirements setting. The original concept for Hawk was a trainer, with the instructor in the rear, and the aircraft was configured accordingly. The decisions to change that use to a display aircraft, carry passengers, and on occasion have instructors in the front seat, had to be complemented by an updated Safety Case, which would highlight the disconnect. It remains to be seen if the Panel's recommendations will be implemented.

On 20 July 2018, four months after Jon's death and three weeks after his evidence to the Panel, Air Officer Commanding 22 Group issued his latest Safety Statement for the Red Arrows to the Chief of the Air Staff. It did not mention stall warning or Command Eject, despite being at the root of the accident and death, respectively.[48]

*

Finally, in his evidence to the Panel, Red 5 revealed that after their pre-flight briefing on the morning of 20 March 2018, Circus Leader Chief Technician William Allen had sought clarification...

'To make sure that if the handle was pulled in the front, the rear seat wouldn't go - which he thought was mad. So we talked about how it was initially designed as a training aircraft and that the instructor would be in the back, so he could take the front seat out. But if the front seat didn't like it and went, the rear potentially could die in the aeroplane.[49]

Precisely.

Three years later...

The family were kept in the dark until the Pre-Inquest Hearing on 14 May 2021; where, as I explained, MoD claimed there had been no systemic failings. This prompted Mr Bayliss to seek progress on, primarily, the recommendation to conduct a feasibility study. He received the following statements:

17 May 2021, from Air Marshal Gray:

'The feasibility of modifying the command ejection system is being re-assessed following the outcome of the 2021 Integrated Review which directed the early retirement of some of the Hawk fleet. Of note, in addition to the enhanced

---

48 AOC22/18/41, 20 July 2018. Red Arrows Safety Statement.
49 Service Inquiry interview with Red 5, 9 April 2018.

training, restrictions have been implemented to limit the circumstances where Circus members or passengers are permitted to fly, reducing the frequency of occupation of the rear-seat during Red Arrows sorties'.

<u>23 June 2021</u>, from the Aviation System Delivery Duty Holder, Group Captain Mark Jackson, Commander UK Hawk Wing:

'A feasibility assessment was completed for both Hawk T.1/1A and T.2. Since that, Air Officer Commanding 22 Group has decided not to pursue Command Eject for the Hawk T2; and the Defence Integrated Review decision to cease 100 Squadron operations (and by default the rest of the "Black fleet") will reduce the number of hours flown in the remaining Service life, which will reduce proportionately the potential benefit that any safety modification would deliver, and the reduction in fleet numbers will make the installation cost per platform higher. T.1/1A however, is to be retained in use with the Red Arrows until at least 2030 and in accordance with the As Low As Reasonably Practicable (ALARP) precautionary principle extension beyond that needs to be considered in any assessment. Ref 2eA [not provided] was therefore updated, with the Operating Duty Holder (AOC 22 Group) ordering a revised Cost Benefit Analysis for T.1A to inform a decision on embodiment, no later than July 2021. It is assessed however, that with mitigation through improved Supernumerary Crew and passenger sortie briefing, restrictions and training processes, operationally necessary flights carrying Supernumerary Crew or passengers with <u>the current command eject system are ALARP and Tolerable</u>.

<u>29 October 2021</u>, from the Coroner's Assistant, forwarding a statement from MoD enclosing a 'Defence Accident Investigation Branch Tracker Report', dated 22 October 2021:

'This recommendation should be closed because part of the Cost Benefit Analysis of installing a Command Ejection system in Hawk T.1 included a feasibility assessment by both BAe Systems and Martin-Baker. The Cost Benefit Analysis concluded that Command Eject implementation would be unlikely to deliver benefit to Hawk T.1/1A based on 2019 assumptions. However, following the Integrated Review decision to cease "Black" Hawk T.1/1A operations from 31 March 2022 the modification programme has been re-focussed on to solely Red Arrows Hawk. Whilst the Cost Benefit Analysis is likely to remain disproportionate, enduring Societal Concern with Red Arrows operations mean <u>the Command Eject safety modification will be taken forward subject to usual programmatic challenges</u>'.

These disjointed missives can be taken a number of ways, but the implication seems to be that the Risk Score is now higher because the Red Arrows undertake most Hawk T.1 flying. Which emphasises something I mentioned earlier. Unique Red Arrows risks were masked by the failure to maintain their Build Standard. One thing is clear. Hanging this on the Integrated Review served to conceal the false declarations that the risk was ALARP.

*

Regarding the Air System Safety Case, Mr Bayliss later questioned the Service Inquiry President as to whether it covered the risks associated with the Red Arrows concept of use and configuration. He replied:

'Without looking at the Air System Safety Case I can't comment'.

He was then asked:

'What risk assessment did you find had been conducted to satisfy MoD that a passenger had sufficient knowledge to make a fit and proper decision to operate the ejection seat, and handle associated stresses in what could be a life threatening situation?'

Replying:

'There were no risk assessments into the carriage of Circus for their roles. And those that were referred to lacked detail in terms of risk assessments for what you've just described. I did not see any and did not request any'.

Yet he had also said of the Safety Case *'All parts were valid'* and had been confident about XX204's airworthiness. Now, he admitted he did not know if an essential prerequisite, assessments of known and long-standing risks to life, even existed. The Coroner instinctively knew Michael had hit the nail, asking:

'Would you have expected there to be some?' [Assessments for passengers].

'That is highly subjective. It would be really difficult to make a risk assessment for that'.

Yet a risk assessment regarding the ejection of rear seat occupants <u>had</u> been made, concluding it was sufficient that the pilot survive.

Having admitted *'The provision of a front seat Command Eject facility may have resulted in both crew surviving'*, it would be rather obvious to MoD that it would face questions on the subject. I can only conclude that a conscious decision was made to avoid the issue with carefully contrived answers. The court was misled.

*

Here, something went very wrong. The delays I have outlined meant the incumbent Air Officer Commanding was long gone before anything was done, and his successor likely had other 'new' problems - not realising that most were the same old problems. In her remarks Air Marshal Gray *'agreed'* with the Panel's recommendations. But to the person tasked with constructing the case for expenditure this is meaningless, except as a minor footnote in the Submission.

Service Inquiry recommendations are allocated an 'owner', the person who must oversee the process to closure. When completed, they are personally signed-off by Director General Defence Safety Authority. But here, the Command Eject recommendation has been closed simply because the feasibility study has been conducted. It was signed-off by Air Marshal Gray in one of her final acts before retiring in January 2022, leaving progress subject to unspecified *'programmatic challenges'*. (On 7 January 2022 Director Military Aviation Authority, Air Vice Marshal Stephen Shell, was promoted and took over from Air Marshal Gray).

A *'will be taken forward'* note in an obscure document does not constitute approval to proceed. It is not even approval to initiate a requirement, never mind a requisition or contract. The new Director General may, in time, ask to review 'open' recommendations, but will he be shown this closed one? He is now the third postholder since the accident, illustrating the lack of continuity and loss of corporate knowledge. But, fortuitously, he was the Director Military Aviation Authority, so it will be clear to him where to begin. Perhaps.

More fundamentally, the Regulatory Set omits the procedures for developing, approving, certifying, producing and embodying modifications. The work is now fragmented - part of the real reason for the delay, not the alleged 3-year feasibility study. In his evidence, Group Captain Jackson claimed safety modifications used to be managed *'individually'*, but are now done *'coherently'* under a 1-Star (Air Commodore). But he was unable to take a further short step back in time, to when all aircraft and equipment modifications were managed *'coherently'* by the specialist HQ Sections I have described; the last of which closed in 1988.

MoD needs to get back to these basics.

*

Since the accident, MoD has engaged consultants in an attempt to resurrect (or construct for the first time) the Air System Safety Case. Their task was thwarted by the lack of an audit trail. This goes back further. After Sean Cunningham's death in 2011, the new Hawk Type

Airworthiness Authority conducted a search for individual aircraft records. Finding nothing in his own files he thought, reasonably, that past records may have been archived to create space. But a thorough search of the RAF Innsworth archives proved fruitless. Astonishingly, not a single reference to Hawk could be found.

It was suggested there may be files in an old lean-to shed behind the Search and Rescue hangar at RAF Valley. And there they languished, water-logged and mouldy as the building was derelict and its roof leaking. A further two weeks was spent searching what remained, but it was mostly 'goo'.[50] Notably, the Nimrod Review had recorded the same thing at BAe Systems, with much of the 'deep archive' held in a room that was flooded on more than one occasion. The Regulatory Authority omitted to say it was fully aware of this, yet presided over recurrence.

My view is that MoD's authorisation to self-regulate on matters of attaining and maintaining airworthiness should be revoked. I do not say this lightly, because the (old) regulations are straight forward and I have seen them work perfectly well. But MoD's persistent refusal to implement them must be dealt with; requiring the matter to be taken out of its hands.

---

50 Telecon (retired) Type Airworthiness Authority/Hill, 26 August 2021.

8. Legal

The Health And Safety at Work Act

The Act imposes two main duties on an employer. The offences are concerned with the creation of a risk of harm and a duty to ensure safety. First, a duty to ensure, so far as is reasonably practicable, the health and safety of all employees. The second extends similar provisions for the protection of those other than employees. There is no limit on the application to other persons. (Sections 2 & 3).

Duties are also imposed on employees, a breach of which involves failure to take reasonable care of himself and of other persons who may be affected by his acts or omissions while at work. Any charge must specify the acts and omissions. (Section 7).

Directors and Managers are liable un Section 37:

'Where an offence committed by a corporate body is proved to have been committed with the consent or connivance of, or to have been attributable to any neglect on the part of, any director, manager, secretary or other similar officer of the body corporate, or a person who was purporting to act in any such capacity, he, as well as the body corporate shall be guilty of that offence ...'.

That is, the entity will have committed an offence under Sections 2 or 3, and the Directors or Managers will be guilty under Section 37.

Section 40 deals with Reasonable Practicability. The defence must prove, on the balance of probabilities, that it was not reasonably practicable to have done more to satisfy the duty. The extent to which the danger was foreseeable is relevant. It is not necessary that anyone was harmed or even put in danger; simply that the possibility existed and the defendants had not done all that was reasonably practicable to prevent it. An entity cannot escape liability by showing that, at a senior level, it had taken steps to ensure safety if, at the operating level, all reasonably practicable steps had not been taken.

The Act is particularly relevant to Red Arrows activities, as the definition of airworthiness includes the safety of those whom the aircraft overflies, and is therefore a matter of public interest. However, the Health and Safety Executive (HSE), charged with overseeing its implementation, is not permitted to involve itself with airworthiness breaches by MoD. It is unclear if this is a self-imposed rule, as it won't discuss the matter except to state its position.[51] Nor is it required to meet the same criteria as the Crown Prosecution Service when making a decision to prosecute.

The distinction between negligence and gross negligence [52]

The very existence of two offences indicates some distinction must be intended. That distinction is not the *kind* of negligence, but *degree* of negligence; so they are not unconnected.

Negligence is commonly defined as *'the inadvertent taking of an unjustifiable risk'*. Whereas, gross negligence is *'a conscious act or omission in disregard of a legal duty and of the consequences to another party'*.[53]

In other words, degree relates to appreciation of the risks involved, together with serious disregard or indifference to an obvious risk. Therefore, gross negligence is a deviation far below the ordinary standard of care, and below even the level of care expected of a careless (negligent) person. Section 1(4)(b) of the Corporate Manslaughter and Corporate Homicide Act 2007 contains this definition:

'A breach of a duty of care by an organisation is a "gross" breach if the conduct alleged to amount to a breach of that duty falls far below what can reasonably be expected of the organisation in the circumstances'.

The outcome (in this case death) is not a factor in determining degree. The question to be asked is:

'Having regard to the risk of death involved, was the conduct of the defendant so bad in all the circumstances as to amount to a criminal act or omission?' [54]

A key test is whether a reasonably prudent person would have foreseen a serious and obvious risk of death arising from the act or omission.

The *Misra* test is important in any decision on grossness and mistakes, the Court of Appeal ruling:

'Mistakes, even very serious mistakes, and errors of judgment, even very serious errors of judgment, are nowhere near enough for a crime as serious as manslaughter to be committed. The defendant's conduct must fall so far below

---

51 HSE letter 7 July 2020, from Jo Anderson, Engagement and Policy Division.
52 'The distinction between gross negligence and recklessness in English criminal law'. Peter Gooderham, School of Law, Manchester University, 2009.
53 Ormerod D. Smith 8 Hogan's Criminal Law (11th edition). Oxford University Press, 2005.
54 *Adomako* [1994] 3 All ER 79.

the standard to be expected of a reasonably competent and careful (person in the defendant's position) that it was something truly exceptionally bad'.[55]

Again, this refers to intent, and the conduct of the individual will always be considered against the background of all the relevant circumstances in which that individual was working. The deliberate overriding or ignoring of systems designed to be safe, and have proven to be safe, may be evidence of grossness.

Duty of Care has no time or geographical limit, and the Judge must impress upon the jury the very high threshold for gross failure. There are many factors the jury must consider, but it is permitted to take into account any other factors which it may consider relevant. For example, evidence of a previous 'near misses', a failure to follow the organisation's own written procedures, and indiscriminate cost cutting, may all be relevant. Also, evidence that the risk was ignored or concealed, or should have been obvious to other individuals within the organisation, would be evidence of gross failings and reckless conduct.

Gross negligence manslaughter [56]

This common law offence applies to an <u>individual</u>, and carries a maximum of life imprisonment. It is committed where the death is a result of a grossly negligent (though otherwise lawful) act or omission on the part of the defendant.

In order to prove the offence the prosecution must establish:

- The defendant owed an existing duty of care to the victim and negligently breached that duty.

- It was reasonably foreseeable that the breach gave rise to a serious and obvious risk of death, and caused the death of the victim.

- The circumstances of the breach were *truly exceptionally bad* and so reprehensible as to justify the conclusion that it amounted to gross negligence and required criminal sanction.

Manslaughter by omission occurs when the omission constitutes a breach of duty to act. The breach does not have to be the only cause of death, nor even the principal cause; but it must have more than minimally, negligibly or trivially caused the death. It is not for the jury

55 *Misra* [2004] EWCA Crim 2375.
56 https://www.cps.gov.uk/legal-guidance/gross-negligence-manslaughter

to evaluate competing causes or to choose which was dominant, provided they are satisfied that the defendant's actions could be said to have been a significant contribution to the victim's death. The President of the Queen's Bench Division:

'The critical ingredients of gross negligence manslaughter (are) the breach of an existing duty of care which it is reasonably foreseeable gives rise to a serious and obvious risk of death and does, in fact, cause death in circumstances where, having regard to the risk of death, the conduct of the defendant was so bad in all the circumstances as to amount to a criminal act or omission'.

So, for example, if a risk to life is properly notified by experts in the field, along with the mitigation required to reduce the risk to ALARP, and this notification rejected, it follows a conscious decision was made. But that does not necessarily constitute an offence, due to the ALARP principle allowing a Cost Benefit Analysis.

But, for example, if the rejection is accompanied by a false declaration, that would be clear evidence of intent. But is not an *'otherwise lawful act'*, so a more serious charge than gross negligence manslaughter would have to be considered.

In the event of litigation, MoD and not the individual would deal with the civil legal consequences. This is because MoD is liable for the acts or omissions of its servants carried out in the course of their employment.

Corporate Manslaughter [57]

Corporate manslaughter is an offence created by Section 1 of the Corporate Manslaughter and Corporate Homicide Act 2007. ('Homicide' relates to Scots Law). It provides that specified government bodies, including MoD, can be prosecuted for corporate manslaughter. The statute provides an exception to the general rule that a Crown body cannot be prosecuted for a criminal offence.

The offence was created to ensure that companies and other organisations can be held properly accountable for serious failings resulting in death. The offence of gross negligence manslaughter was abolished insofar as it related to companies and other organisations. Within the framework of the Act, the failings of a number of individuals may be aggregated.

---

57 https://www.cps.gov.uk/legal-guidance/corporate-manslaughter

The effect was to widen the scope of the offence so that the focus is now on the overall management of the organisation's activities, rather than the actions of particular individuals. The test for liability is essentially the same as for gross negligence manslaughter. However, it is no longer necessary to show that a person who was the 'controlling mind' of the organisation was personally responsible. Wider considerations such as the overall management of health and safety, the selection and training of staff, the implementation of systems of working, and the supervision of staff, can be taken into account.

An organisation is not liable if the failings were exclusively at a junior level. The failings of senior management must have formed a substantial element in the breach. However, failings at senior level do not of themselves have to amount to a gross breach of duty. Liability for the offence is assessed by looking at the failings as a whole.

'An organisation to which this section applies is guilty of an offence if the way in which its activities are managed or organised:

- *Causes a person's death, and;*
- *Amounts to a gross breach of a relevant duty of care owed by the organisation to the deceased'.*

The following needs to be proved:

- The defendant is a qualifying organisation.
- The organisation owed a relevant duty of care to the deceased.
- There was a gross breach of that duty by the organisation.
- The way in which its activities were managed or organised by its senior management was a substantial element in the breach.
- The gross breach caused or more than minimally contributed to the death.

It is not necessary to prove that there was a serious and obvious risk of death. Nor, that individuals were reckless to the safety of others. Applicability is as described above in the gross negligence section.

As MoD is an inanimate body which does not have the capacity to foresee risk, the penalty must be a fine. The level depends on the size of the organisation, and ranges from £180,000 to £20M. Quite how this would deter a Department of State is unclear.

Senior management

Section 1(4) of the Act states:

'Senior management, in relation to an organisation, means the persons who play significant roles in:

- *The making of decisions about how the whole or a substantial part of its activities are to be managed or organised, or;*

- *The actual managing or organising of the whole or a substantial part of those activities'.*

This includes executives and managers at the top of the organisation, and could also encompass, for example, anyone whose work constituted *'a substantial part'* of the activities of the organisation.

Thus, given the structure and system of delegation in MoD, this is not restricted to Military Aviation Authority's Duty Holder construct. Anyone with (e.g.) airworthiness delegation is a duty holder; and everyone has a duty to report potential hazards or risks, and violations. I mentioned the key role of Technical Agencies in verifying the attainment of airworthiness, and its maintenance; therefore they play a substantial part in this, whereas senior Duty Holders may have no direct input at all. In this sense, Technical Agencies are *de facto* 'senior' duty holders, and their competence certainly of far greater import within the Safety Management System.

The focus of this element is on *'the way in which activities are managed or organised by senior management'.* A one-off failure may not suffice, but unchecked systemic failings are likely to be more relevant. Where the prosecution is relying on a series of failings over a period of time, the question of whether the deceased would have survived but for the gross breach may require careful analysis of the timeline to identify the time and circumstances in which the gross breach was operative, and whether intervention at that time would have avoided death. Here, the issue is clear-cut. MoD has admitted the breaches, and the evidence shows that senior staff were directly and deeply involved. While I have cited a few examples at 2- and 4-Star levels, a more comprehensive body of evidence is available in the main submissions to the Nimrod and Mull of Kintyre Reviews.[58]

---

58 https://sites.google.com/site/militaryairworthiness/their-greatest-disgrace-2016

9. The Coroner's Inquest

The Coroner's Court is a court of inquiry, not a court of litigation. The Inquest is a fact-finding exercise, and the Coroner's role is to find facts based on the evidence heard (not the evidence submitted). Like Judges, Coroners can declare 'facts' even though provided with evidence that they are not facts. That is, there exists judicial truth and actual truth. The proceedings closely resemble that of a civil case, but the Coroner may sit alone or call a jury. Coroners are prohibited by law from attributing blame. The standard of proof is 'balance of probabilities'.

An Inquest is usually opened, and then adjourned until MoD finishes its investigations. The technical investigation is often completed years after the Service Inquiry, and there are usually conflicts between them. (Here, the Technical Report has not been released). MoD is allowed to withhold, conceal or deny the existence of germane evidence, so the starting point is balanced in its favour. Lacking the resources to employ independent investigators or experts who can identify what is missing, this places the Coroner and families at a disadvantage.

Coroners face a dilemma. They have a duty to assist the investigator. A balancing act is required to ensure the cause of the accident is not completely ignored in the quest for cause of death - given one often leads to the other. The most important consideration is recurring failures. In a civil case, if the Coroner fails in this duty the investigator (the Air Accidents Investigation Branch) must put its interests second to the Coroner's, risking recurrence. But in military cases the investigator is also the regulator, user and final arbiter. That is, if the Coroner assists MoD, recurrence becomes almost a certainty.

*

The Crown Prosecution Guide for Coroners states:

> 'It is the general duty of every citizen (under common law) to attend an Inquest if they are in possession of any information or evidence that details how a person came to their death'.

Plainly, one doesn't just pitch up and ask to be heard. One reports the information to the Coroner; but there is no impartial mechanism to test its relative merits, except to hear it in court. In practice, a Coroner will invite MoD to comment on evidence, and by default it will reject the adverse. And so MoD determines the direction of the Inquest.

Who can families turn to for the truth? No police force has ever conducted a full investigation into the circumstances surrounding a military aircraft accident. And, following the Sean Cunningham case the Independent Office for Police Conduct ruled that Lincolnshire Police were correct to say that someone who was not an affected party was 'not permitted' to report a crime, and the force was under no duty to investigate.[59] That leaves families to conduct their own investigation, but they have no right of access to evidence or witnesses. Faced with the full and combined might of Departments of State - MoD, Home Office and Justice (and Work and Pensions in the case of the Health and Safety Executive) - the bereaved often feel *they* are in the dock. And in such a labyrinthine system, these departments find it easy to pass the buck. In reality this is a mutual support system, the aim being to avoid obligations. As, for example, the Crown Office in Scotland did in the Chinook ZD576 (Mull of Kintyre) case, when stating it was for the Metropolitan Police to investigate because the offences were committed in London.[60] The Met did not reply to a formal complaint, so the 29 deaths remain to be investigated.[61]

Here, the correct issues relating to cause of death were submitted to the Coroner (and police), but no witnesses were called and evidence detrimental to MoD was disregarded. Of note, the Oxfordshire and Wiltshire Coroners (Nimrod XV230 and Hercules XV179, respectively) have previously accepted the *same* evidence and engaged with the *same* witnesses; illustrating that some are perfunctory, some thorough. Others regard themselves as the only authority capable of conducting a complex technical investigation. The very worst openly act with the State against the bereaved, as in the Sea King ASaC Mk7 case.

Submission to the Senior Coroner for North West Wales

On 17 October 2019 I sent the following to Mr Dewi Pritchard-Jones:

> *The RAF Service Inquiry report into this accident was published in a redacted form last week. It reveals MoD failures repeating those which led to the death of Red Arrows pilot Flight Lieutenant Sean Cunningham in November 2011*

---

59 *Inter alia*, e-mail 20 November 2019 14:12 from IOPC.
60 Crown Office & Procurator Fiscal Service letter LP-4, 8 November 2016.
61 Formal complaint letter to Metropolitan Police, 29 November 2016.

at RAF Scampton, Lincolnshire. For example:

- *No common training objectives, lack of continuation training, and failure to record training*
- *Improper recording of maintenance actions*
- *Red Arrows adopted different procedures to other Hawk squadrons*
- *Risks not tolerable and As Low As Reasonably Practicable*
- *Inaccuracy and ambiguity of publications, and failure of MoD to disseminate publications and information*
- *Quality Assurance and authorisation failures compromising Air Safety*
- *Pressure arising from overworked aircrew/increased tempo/lack of resources*

The death of Corporal Bayliss is a recurrence. Only the final act differs. I hope, therefore, this short note helps you achieve your aim of preventing recurrence'.

I copied this to the Lincolnshire Coroner. Neither replied. On 19 March 2020 I sought acknowledgement of receipt. Again, no reply. Mr Pritchard-Jones then retired, and on 30 March 2021 I wrote to Acting Senior Coroner Katie Sutherland. And again on 7 April 2021. Still no reply. So, while there is a *'general duty'* to come forward with evidence, it would seem Coroners are not obliged to even acknowledge receipt.

*

On 23 October 2019, Mr Pritchard-Jones had been reminded that the Operating Duty Holder must sign a Safety Statement to the effect that all risks are As Low As Reasonably Practicable (ALARP). His reply was unsatisfactory, stating that only questions relating to authorisation and whether it was essential to carry passengers would be addressed:

'The other matters are beyond the scope of the Inquest and are matters to be dealt with by the MoD'.[62]

This was palpably wrong. The main question mark was over the Command Eject ALARP statement, Regulatory Article 1210(2) stating:

'The validity of an ALARP argument can only be decided definitively by the courts, in the event of an accident'.

This has never happened at any court, leaving the bereaved in a legal limbo, unable to get at the truth. But Mr Pritchard-Jones had gone

---

62 E-mail Pritchard-Jones/Jones, 29 October 2019 11:42.

further, in 2016 making his views on military Inquests clear:

'One could argue that Inquests into military deaths are rather pointless a. ̦ˠ *merely regurgitate what has already been made known at the military inquiry'.*

This might explain his refusal to hold a mandatory Inquest into the death of Flight Lieutenant Hywel Poole, killed in a Tornado mid-air collision in 2012. MoD had failed in its duty to inform him that Hywel had been repatriated to North Wales, at which point he could perhaps plead ignorance. But he still did not act after being informed by members of the public and Hywel's family. Justice, and application of the law, should not be a postcode lottery, relying on the moral rectitude of the Coroner and his/her willingness to hold a Department of State to account. It is yet to be seen if Ms Sutherland will hold an Inquest.

Worth noting is that after the Oxfordshire Coroner, the admirable Andrew Walker, severely criticised MoD at the Nimrod XV230 Inquest in May 2008, the Government sought to curtail Coroners' powers by having military Inquests held behind closed doors. The proposed changes to the law stalled, but one cannot help but observe that Mr Pritchard-Jones' stance is very close to this. The public weren't to be excluded, but its narrow scope, and the refusal to call or heed relevant witnesses, meant they may as well have been. Its aims became impossible to achieve. I do not believe any Coroner would risk such a prejudiced action without higher approval. The answer may lie in the Chief Coroner's refusal to reply to expressions of concern.[63]

The Article 2 question

Article 2(1) of the European Convention of Human Rights places two substantive duties on member states: an obligation to refrain from taking life, and an obligation to safeguard life. This is modified by an additional layer of 'operational duty', asking whether an employer knew, or ought to have known, of a real and immediate risk to the life of an individual, and if it failed to take measures to mitigate that risk. (It can be seen there is a consistency between all these legal issues, which is as it should be).

Article 2 Inquests are enhanced Inquests held in cases where *'the State or its agents have failed to protect the deceased against a human threat or other risk'.* The crucial difference is that, in an Article 2 Inquest, not only does

---

63 Letter to His Honour Judge Thomas Teague QC, 1 July 2021.

the cause of death have to be established, but also the broader circumstances surrounding the death.

Article 2 <u>must</u> be invoked if it appears to be arguable on the evidence that these substantive duties have been breached. But arguable on what evidence? What MoD deigns to offer the court? Only rarely is sufficient known by the families or public to be able to submit the facts.

Nevertheless, applicability to military personnel is clear. Senior Coroner for Oxfordshire, Darren Salter, relating to his Inquest into an RAF Puma helicopter accident on 11 October 2015:

'The Inquest sits alongside the Service Inquiry, is held in open court and is independent. It involves the participation of families/interested persons. There is the opportunity to see documents and question witnesses. Also to make submissions to me. Further, the Inquest can look for lessons to be learned. In a case where Article 2 applies, as in this case, the question of how a person came by his or her death is extended to also include the circumstances'.

And Lord Alexander Philip, in his 2009 Mull of Kintyre Review:

'A Board of Inquiry was an internal process convened for the Armed Services to determine how a serious incident happened and why, and to make recommendations to prevent a recurrence. The Board of Inquiry was not a substitute for a legal inquiry into cause and circumstances of death'.

Despite being notified of serious and recurring breaches, their direct relationship with cause of death, and reminded of the above decisions, Mr Pritchard-Jones ruled this was <u>not</u> to be an Article 2 Inquest.

*

On 20 April 2021, the representatives of the pilot agreed to the Bayliss family taking the lead on Article 2. Nevertheless, they made an excellent submission to the Coroner listing a number of potential breaches:

1. *'Inadequate guidance promulgated to Red Arrows pilots regarding the execution of the relevant manoeuvre, specifically in relation to:*

   - *The minimum height for the initiation of the final turn (i.e. 1400 feet - a recommendation which was contained in FTP3225H, Issue 1, dated January 2018, which was not a mandated Red Arrows reference document, and of which Flt Lt Stark was not aware);*

   - *The minimum gliding speed with landing gear down (which had been increased from 165/170 knots to 170/175 kts in 1995 to "increase safety margins" in relation to a potential stall, but then had been reduced again to 165/170 knots in 2002 without apparent explanation);*

- *The safe limits of angle of bank within the final turn of a PEFATO (as to which the Service Inquiry panel found that there was no guidance);*
- *Objective measures/gates for the relevant manoeuvre generally to ensure safe execution.*
- *The minimum height at which to initiate a go-around;*
- *Contract information where the pilot intends to perform a go-around;*

2. *Inadequate training provided to Red Arrows pilots regarding the execution of the relevant manoeuvre, specifically in relation to:*

- *All items above;*
- *Warning signs of impending aerodynamic stall, particularly in relation to the lack of the cardinal warning sign - i.e. buffet - in circumstances where a smoke pod is attached to the aircraft;*
- *Standard Stall Recovery.*

3. *Inadequate information promulgated to Red Arrows pilots regarding the performance of Hawk T.1, insofar as its handling is affected by:*

- *Weight of various components added to the "clean" aircraft, in particular the weight of the smoke pod;*
- *Speed differences consequent upon variation in aircraft all up mass;*
- *Directly linked to above - differences in stall margins consequent upon variation in aircraft all up mass.*

4. *Inadequacies of the document set relating to Hawk T.1 (that was current and had been promulgated to Red Arrows pilots as at 20 March 2018) relating to:*

- *The lack of information and/or conflicting information relevant to the items (1) and (3) above (as identified by the Service Inquiry panel);*
- *The lack of updating of the document set to reflect the significant increase in basic Hawk T.1 aircraft weight over time (leading to an erosion of safety margins);*
- *The lack of updating of the Operating Data Manual - the ODM in use as at 20 March 2018 had not been updated since 1998 and contained no reference at all to a smoke pod, nor any data for a Hawk T.1 of the same weight and fit as XX204'.*[64]

---

64 Submissions for a Pre-Inquest Review Hearing on behalf of Flight Lieutenant David

It can be seen this covers, in admirable detail, one of the common factors identified from XX177 (2011) and other accidents - the failure (in fact, refusal) to disseminate publications and information.

Pre-Inquest Hearing

On 14 May 2021, a Pre-Inquest Hearing was held in Caernarfon, conducted by Ms Sutherland. I have already mentioned that Edward Pleeth QC, representing MoD, claimed there were <u>no systemic failings</u>. This was known to be wrong by anyone familiar with the previous Red Arrows fatality (Sean Cunningham), never mind numerous other deaths. Similarly, at the Sea King Inquest mentioned earlier MoD immediately claimed the aircraft were serviceable and airworthy, despite the Board of Inquiry spelling out why they were not. The mendacity leaves families flummoxed.

However, Ms Sutherland was now aware that false statements had been recklessly made in her court, and the family misled. That, MoD's obligation to be candid in matters of fact had been disregarded. This is a crime against the justice system itself, as it prevents courts from establishing the truth. While initially reaffirming Mr Pritchard-Jones' Article 2 ruling, she said she would keep matters under review.

*

On 23 June 2021, the Delivery Duty Holder, Group Captain Mark Jackson, submitted a statement to the Coroner. While I had received no reply to my brief submission, Ms Sutherland had clearly read it and asked MoD to comment on any potential or established links between XX204 and other Hawk T.1/1A accident causes. At paragraph 3c, under 'Previous accidents', Jackson listed only two, from 2011 (XX177 and XX179), in which the pilots were killed. He said:

'There is no overlap between the cause of (XX177) and that of XX204'.

The truth, of course, was very different, and easily gleaned by comparing the two reports. And no mention was made of another accident I will discuss later, in which there was not only overlap, but the causes of accident and death were identical.

At this point, what confidence could Ms Sutherland have that she was being told the whole truth? MoD had already proven itself a highly

---

Stark. (Charlotte Law, 20 April 2020).

unreliable witness, and was now denying the content of its own reports. It was now her turn to be flummoxed.

*

I spoke to Gayle, Jon's sister. It bothered me that, apparently, the family's solicitor was not pursuing this. It transpired they were no longer represented. MoD had settled out of court, so *pro bono* legal assistance ceased. This, and seeking to draw out the subsequent process in the hope families find it too expensive, is a common MoD tactic.

I was also informed by her father, Michael, that Mr Pleeth had approached him pledging he would ensure *'everything was okay'*. But he was there to represent MoD, not the family or any serviceman. This artifice had also been visited upon the Cunningham family in 2018.

Further submissions

Gayle and Michael declared to the Coroner that I was their technical advisor, and that she should take any submission from me, copied to the family, as being *from* the family. Ms Sutherland acknowledged this.

On 14 October 2021 a list of witnesses was provided, and the family invited to comment on how the Inquest should proceed. Michael called me the following day to discuss how he should reply. On 17 October he wrote to the Coroner, reflecting on my 2019 submission:

'I note that the respective MoD reports list at least 12 common factors. All are related to safety. This makes me wonder if MoD can demonstrate the Hawk T.1 was airworthy in January 2018. Importantly, in my son's case, was the Air System Safety Case valid? Did one even exist? I would respectfully ask you to put these questions to MoD. I would also ask you to note that precisely the same systemic failings were recorded by Sir Charles Haddon-Cave in his Nimrod Review (2009). The recurrences and the failure of the MoD to act on the recommendations of previous Coroner's Courts constitute manslaughter. The risks to pilot and passenger were not As Low As Reasonably Practicable'.

In reply, on 20 October the Coroner confirmed:

'Insofar as the questions for the MoD I can put these to the witnesses for you at the Inquest but I should also inform you that you and any other family members will have the opportunity to put any questions to the witnesses relative to the scope of the Inquest, should you wish'.

Michael and I spoke again. He was curious about one witness, a Group Captain (Jackson) described only as a 'duty holder'. What does that mean to the man on the street? What was he responsible for? Would he be able to answer pertinent questions? Few MoD witnesses can; perfectly illustrated at the Hercules XV179 Inquest in Trowbridge on 15 October 2008, when the aircraft Integrated Project Team Leader, also a Group Captain, answered incorrectly a series of questions relating to his airworthiness, risk and safety management responsibilities.

My concern, however, was that the Operating Duty Holder, AOC 22 Group, was not on the list. The balance had been tipped, by the Coroner, further towards MoD. I suggested that the key objective now must be to persuade her that the evidence submitted met the Article 2 criteria. That, we keep it simple by only referring to violations MoD had already admitted. Between us we crafted a reply, submitted on 25 October:

'Submission that Article 2 be invoked

I submit to you that some of the objections raised by MoD's Counsel, Edward Pleeth QC, for not invoking Article 2 are blatantly untrue and misleading.

(1) Mr Pleeth claims that the MoD chain of command did not know of the risk(s). The Service Inquiry report identified and recommended changes that had already been recommended at previous Inquests and in Service Inquiry reports, both in the Red Arrows and the wider RAF. Most are safety related and/or systemic. Indeed, the RAF Director of Flight Safety is on record from the early 1990s putting senior RAF officers on notice of the failings identified by the Service Inquiry.[65] Clearly the MoD has failed to implement the recommendations.

(2) Witness statements and the Service Inquiry report make it clear that many of the factors identified are root causes which, if removed, would have prevented the outcome.

(3) These recurring and systemic failings of a dysfunctional and, I believe, culpable nature are such that they need to be recorded in your final report, so that lessons may be learned; in accordance with the Chief Coroner's Guidance'.

We could only wait, but in a final attempt before the Inquest reopened I wrote on 30 October 2021 reiterating that the Service Inquiry had spelt out systemic failings in detail, noting:

'It is a fundamental principle of accident investigation that one never simply blames the final act. Here, MoD has been unable to demonstrate the

---

65 Specifically, RAF Chief Engineer Air Chief Marshal Sir Michael Alcock, and the Assistant Chief of the Air Staff Air Vice Marshal (later Air Chief Marshal Sir) Anthony Bagnall.

airworthiness of the Hawk T.1 fleet for many years - something admitted in the Cunningham case, and which got even worse by 2018. Perhaps you might consider asking why MoD has had such great difficulty reconstructing an Air System Safety Case, or indeed a Whole Aircraft Safety Case'.

For the first time in the two years since my initial submission, I received a reply. On 1 November, the day before the Inquest was due to open, Ms Sutherland said briefly:

'As with all Inquests where a full investigation has been conducted the outcomes and findings therefrom will be addressed and evidence heard accordingly'.

I replied, pointing out there had been no *'full investigation'*:

'Internal investigations exclude the bereaved and other interested parties. If an Inquest only addresses evidence from that investigation, then it cannot possibly meet any obligation to prevent recurrence. As you have been informed that relevant evidence was withheld from MoD's investigators, and concealed from the family, will that evidence, also sent to your predecessor, now be heard for the first time?' [66]

Unlike her predecessor, Ms Sutherland was open-minded and later incorporated my points into her decision. (It may well be that she would have anyway, but it was imperative she be reminded).

*

Ms Sutherland made another ruling. Audio recordings of proceedings would not be made available to the public, only interested parties. Yet that same week the Lincolnshire Coroner agreed again to provide recordings of the 2014 Cunningham Inquest; this time for a substantially reduced price than quoted to myself in 2018 (£264); but still well above the £5 laid down by the Chief Coroner. Michael notified Ms Sutherland that he required copies, receiving them free of charge on 7 February 2022; but only the November 2021 proceedings.

Today, audio recordings have replaced stenographers. The Chief Coroner's Guidance #4 requires them to be kept for a minimum of 15 years, so it rather follows they must be intelligible. Here, they were dreadful. Worse, families are expected to pay to have them transcribed. For example, after the Sea King ASaC Mk7 Inquest in 2007, the mother of Lieutenant Marc Lawrence RN was quoted £3,700 by the Oxford Coroner's Office for a 4-day Inquest.

---

66 E-mail Hill/Sutherland, 1 November 2021 11:52.

To coin a phrase, this is *truly exceptionally bad*. In both cases I transcribed them as best I could, but the questions put by Gayle and her husband Matthew are heavily distorted, and the Coroner's paper-rustling drowns out many witness replies. (The Sea King recordings are exactly the same). It cannot be said, therefore, that a full record of the Inquest exists. This is where the Coroners Service needs to apply a little lateral thinking. They have the recording equipment, but don't know how to use it. Ask someone.

The proceedings

A lie is a statement that is known or intended to be misleading, inaccurate, or false. It is compounded if the liar has a duty to others who rely on the truthfulness of the statement and, especially, if there are harmful consequences. Lying by omission occurs when a person leaves out important information, or fails to correct a misconception.

*

The Inquest reopened on 2 November 2021. Ms Sutherland had put Michael's submissions to MoD, who had replied with further disclosure (i.e. admitting the submissions were correct). Rejecting its previous claim there were no systemic failings, or overlap between this and the Cunningham case in 2011, she stated:

> *The threshold has been met for Article 2 to be engaged due to breaches in duties. There are <u>systemic</u> issues surrounding, for example, the training, the guidance to pilots and engineers, information sharing, both as contributory and aggravating factors; which I don't consider, having taken all the evidence into account, to be more active than negligence'.*

Ms Sutherland also said that *'all evidence had been provided to interested parties'* and, having taken it all *'into account'*, she had determined there was no *'wilful misconduct'*.

That is, MoD's actions were negligent, but not to a gross degree. These breaches, she said, were linked to *'deficiencies in the regulatory framework'*. While it is true the current regulations are not yet up to the standard of the pre-2010 ones (which she didn't mention), this was not the main deficiency. That lay in implementation. Nevertheless, this was a positive step forward.

Ms Sutherland came to this decision before hearing any witness evidence, and knowing MoD had not disclosed all the evidence. Other evidence would emerge only after MoD's claims were fact-checked.

It was therefore unclear how MoD's violations would be dealt with. As the Coroner knew ALARP statements were false, and hence the importance of the correct Duty Holder being present and being asked the correct questions, the only reasonable conclusion is that senior officers were being protected. This set the tone.

The Coroner finished her opening statement by promising the family a *'full and frank Inquiry'* into Jon's death. But that is only achievable if the court is told truth. It wasn't, and so her promise could not be kept.

I have no intention of dissecting the evidence of the witnesses in detail. All were military personnel and most of the evidence was unrelated to the main root cause of death. I will instead concentrate on that of Group Captain Jackson, the final witness.

Evidence of Group Captain Mark Jackson

In her opening, Ms Sutherland had stated to MoD's Mr Pleeth that she expected Group Captain Jackson to answer questions on *'overlapping recommendations'* between this accident and those of 2011. The family expected this to be the common Factors which formed the basis of her Article 2 decision. Mr Pleeth replied *'Group Captain Jackson has come prepared to answer all the questions'*.

But upon taking the stand on Day 3, Jackson made it clear he would <u>not</u> be answering questions about events prior to him taking up post in July 2020; only about what was being done now, nearly four years after the accident. Very clearly, in the interim the implications of the Article 2 decision, and having to answer questions about why systemic failings had been allowed to persist (despite stating to the Lincolnshire Coroner in 2014 that they were being dealt with) had dawned on MoD.

Despite this negating her opening statement, her promise to the family, and the basis upon which the Inquest proceeded, the Coroner allowed this. Yet the regulations governing Jackson's appointment state:

'It is essential that Risk Assessments are reviewed with the changeover of accountable individuals'.[67]

And, as Delivery Duty Holder, he was required to provide the Operating

---

67 Defence Safety Authority DSA01.2, chapter 3.29.

Duty Holder with *'relevant subject matter advice'.*[68] Was *he* satisfied with the same reply when asking the same questions at his regular reviews? (If he was, that would explain much). Jackson would be aware that MoD's aim was to avoid answering questions about inconsistencies in its evidence. Most importantly, it did not want the Operating Duty Holder appearing in court. To make such an about turn he must have been confident he had top cover, including from the Coroner.

Having been told to ask certain questions of Jackson, the family had not asked them of other witnesses. They were left high and dry. This can be summed up in one early exchange, when Michael asked about the status of risk assessments for Circus at the time of the accident. The Coroner interjected:

'It is very difficult for Group Captain Jackson to answer that on the basis he wasn't in post at that time'.

Later, Gayle asked a similar question regarding documentation, and was told that this was not for Group Captain Jackson, but the Service Inquiry President; who had appeared earlier and declined to answer the same question. (See chapter 6). He was not recalled.

Plainly, this change of agreed scope had been agreed privately with the Coroner at some point between Day 1 and Day 3. What, then, is the point of an Inquest into a 2018 death if no questions are allowed on events before July 2020? This is so perverse, it could be argued as grounds for reopening the Inquest. What could the family do? It would take great presence of mind, but one course of action might be to immediately walk out and beckon the press to follow. They would have nothing to lose as they had been left with nowhere else to go.

*

Jackson's evidence lasted more than four hours, mostly spent walking the Coroner through progress on the Panel's 25 recommendations - in the same way the President had taken her through his Factors. The danger in such an approach is that it assumes all the Factors have been identified and categorised correctly - which they had not. Similarly, that the recommendations cover all the failures, breaches and violations, which they did not. His evidence was mostly a series of statements of intent to begin doing what senior staff and his predecessors had declared many times to have been done already. He was well rehearsed

---

68 Regulatory Instruction MAA/RI/DG/02/10, paragraph 5c.

and presented as knowledgeable.

Matters were different when out of this comfort zone; nowhere more evident than when he claimed the Nimrod Review of 2007-9 had led to a *'root and branch review of the Military Aviation Authority'* - formed in April 2010 as a result of the Review. While few in MoD are taught the truth - it is simply too embarrassing, and the MAA itself has made this claim - this underscores that lacking corporate memory mistakes will be repeated. It becomes impossible to understand what has *not* been done.

The Coroner should have insisted someone accountable appeared. But MoD selects its witnesses carefully for their presentational skills. Their lack of subject knowledge is irrelevant. In fact, to MoD this is a necessity. Families are powerless, because the subject is understood by few, even in MoD. And those few are quite definitely excluded as witnesses. They are not even allowed to be part of the briefing chain.

What Group Captain Jackson proposed, in so many words, was that MoD starts implementing its own policies. While he could perhaps influence this at the Central Flying School (although that would require him to understand past failures), he had no say whatsoever across the wider RAF or MoD. But the Coroner deferred to his rank. Her mistake was not taking him through the 12 common factors with XX177. Put another way, she based her decision to declare an Article 2 Inquest on admitted systemic failings, yet rejected any attempt to discuss them.

Given this procedural decision was only made known after she opened the Inquest, and just two weeks after providing the witness list, once again the family had no opportunity to react. Common sense dictates that MoD should have been instructed to produce witnesses who could answer questions on the failings. If that meant a short delay, so be it. Alternatively, the evidence of other witnesses could have been condensed, as much of it was irrelevant to the cause of death.

*

Only the family focussed on the issues that would explain Jon's death. They were fobbed off with 'initiatives' that are so fundamental they are (or were) hammered into MoD recruits during induction training.

Nevertheless, an excellent attempt was made by Flight Lieutenant Stark's representative to uncover why crucial information had not been circulated. Jackson simply replied that RAF Standards and Evaluation were responsible for publications; which will surprise any Publications Authority. He was talking about what happens at the air station or squadron. He omitted, or perhaps did not understand, that this small final part of the chain relies on the Build Standard being maintained. I emphasise this, because (a) it was not, and (b) doing so would have prevented Jon's death. It is the basic process underpinning the safety of all in-service equipment and its use, yet it is not even mentioned in the Regulatory Set. That must be the starting point for any action, but was beyond the ken or the gift of the witness.

This failure to disseminate information repeats the worst failings in the Cunningham case. There, Martin-Baker were prosecuted for not providing information. Despite the Judge naming an MoD official who had signed for it (Mr Barry Cowell), the company pleaded guilty to avoid a court case and were fined £1.1M. The real failure was not addressed, and Jon was the next victim.

*

The Coroner asked what risk training took place. Jackson said there were *'several courses'*, including the short Duty Holder course at which the use of Bow-Ties was explained. The Coroner replied, *'Has the system stayed the same but Bow-Tie been added?'* An excellent question (and again revealing she had read submissions from the public), as there exists a notion that Bow-Ties *are* Risk Management. He responded *'I can't say if the system has changed'*. And therein lies a recurring problem. A brief course is inadequate except as an overview, or a refresher after long, practical experience. It does not make you an expert. Fine, if you have real experts to call upon. He didn't.

Regarding these courses, DSA01.2 ('Implementation of Defence Policy for Health, Safety and Environmental Protection'), requires:

> *'All Duty Holders who have been in post for more than 3 months should hold a valid Defence Safety Authority approved Duty Holder Course certificate; and those with less than 3 months in post should be able to demonstrate that appropriate action has been taken to attend a Defence Safety Authority approved Duty Holder Course within 3 months of appointment'.*

Prior to July 2011 one must have attended the Duty Holder Air Safety Course prior to taking up appointment. A significant difference. Three months doesn't sound long, but is a large part of a typical two-year posting. (Group Captain Jackson moved on not long after the Inquest, his tour lasting significantly less than two years). We've already learned that Supernumerary Crew could not receive *their* mandated safety training for almost two years before the accident. The *'appropriate action'* was taken (trying to book a place), but they remained untrained. Relative priorities need to be established. What is more important? Safety training to mitigate risk to life to the trainee; or a Group Captain, Air Vice Marshal or Air Chief Marshal receiving a short presentation on a subject where they are not required to answer for their actions?

Context is required. The typical high turnover rate of postholders means training courses are usually over-subscribed. When I took up my first Service HQ post in August 1985, I was required to attend certain courses. But if I could not (and I couldn't, having been given 5 days' notice of posting), after six months I was deemed to have gained sufficient knowledge through on-the-job experience - which proved to be a fair assumption. However, my appointment was predicated on having at least 10 years relevant experience aimed at eventually holding such a position. I emphasise therefore that no criticism is intended of Group Captain Jackson or any of his staff.

*

On the one occasion cause of death was broached (although not expressed as such), Jackson replied that a feasibility study had been carried out into whether the Command Eject system could be changed so pilots in the front seat could eject a passenger: *'(It) was completed by Martin-Baker and it was deemed, yes, it could be incorporated into the aircraft'*. He reported that the improvements would take *'between two and three years once the business case is approved'*.

Even if we overlook that this implies nobody recognised the risk until March 2018 (demonstrably wrong, witness the Red Arrows Risk Register post-XX177 in 2011, which he did not refer to), did a feasibility study really take over three years? Martin-Baker knew exactly what was needed - confirmed to me separately by two of their retired engineers. It is inconceivable they have not advised and even lobbied MoD to embody this change, beginning in the mid-70s when it was known the Red Arrows would be adopting Hawk.

Of wider concern, and symptomatic of MoD's ills, *'Business Case'* has replaced 'Board Submission'. From the Nimrod Review:

'There was a shift in culture and priorities towards "business" and financial targets, at the expense of functional values such as safety and airworthiness. The shortcomings in the current airworthiness system are manifold and include a Safety Culture that has allowed "business" to eclipse airworthiness'.

I would go further. MoD's Safety Management System has been

corrupted from the top down by this business culture.

*

There followed an odd exchange led by Ms Charlotte Law, representing Flight Lieutenant Stark, about situational awareness and when Hawk T.1 was fitted with GPS. Asked to confirm GPS had been available for *'over 25 years'*, Group Captain Jackson replied *'It is definitely not that old'*. Pilots had flown with it before Gulf War 1 (1991). To be fair, few of Jackson's age would be expected to know the answer, and it was unclear what point was being made. But, for example, GPS must not be used as the primary navigation aid, so is often not fully integrated within navigation systems. Its critical function is that of providing Time of Day to system clocks (e.g. for encryption).

Regarding a 2007 recommendation to fit a stall warner, Ms Law asked why it had not been progressed. Jackson replied: *'I do not know that. I cannot answer'*. MoD's Mr Pleeth complained again that *'questions about what went before cannot be answered by Group Captain Jackson'*. Strangely, given her previous stance, Ms Sutherland rejected this, saying it was a *'fair'* question and Ms Law should continue. But her reasoning later became clear - she had plainly pre-judged the case and decided this was to be one of her two matters of concern. (Explained later).

Jackson simply replied that he could not *'speak of risk'*. Yet he was there, allegedly, to tell the court about the mitigation of risks set out by the Panel in its recommendations. As Delivery Duty Holder, his entire job revolved around understanding the risks he was carrying.

The Coroner briefly opened the door, but who would be able to advise Ms Law what to say next? MoD's obstruction made it impossible for her. And surely it is for the Coroner to ask the obvious question - *Well, who can speak of risk?* Especially as the Inquest was brought about by complete failure of the Risk Management process.

Group Captain Jackson told the court he was in charge, but 'his' risk mitigation must fail scrutiny. The mandated Requirement Scrutiny Instructions list 39 questions.[69] (If you like, the *39 Steps* to ensuring a spend against the Defence budget is 'good', and the primary means of avoiding waste). Not all are applicable to every requirement, but lacking

---

69 For example, AUS(FS)/474 of 1 January 1988, reflecting the Permanent Under-Secretary of State's directive that *'all procurement expenditure is dependent on a requirement which has been approved by the appropriate authority on PUS's behalf'*.

the information requested by Ms Law one would be unable to progress beyond #1 - *'Why is it needed?'* - a question that must be answered with a summary of the background, including previous attempts to acquire the same capability. Precisely what he was asked in court, and he should have been required to answer. If unable to do so, on what basis can he be confident his proposed actions will succeed? Recurrence is inevitable. As it was in 2011, and again in 2018.

Am I being unfair? Witnesses take an oath to tell *the truth, the whole truth and nothing but the truth.* But what if a witness is selected because he doesn't know the truth? Group Captain Jackson's appearance did nothing to further the aims of the Inquest.

Tomorrow, remember yesterday

Michael asked about Jon's GoPro camera and mobile phone, and the data on them. The Service Inquiry report, as released to the family, did not mention the devices. Chief Technician William Allen confirmed Jon had both, and had filmed at least the outward leg to RAF Valley on the GoPro; and was seen to have it on his wrist just before the accident flight. But asked by the Coroner, Mr Pleeth QC stated firmly:

'The Defence Safety Authority is in possession of a smoke damaged phone <u>and GoPro, <u>neither of which are retrievable in any way</u></u>'.

The Coroner and family were clearly expected to accept this as fact. Unhappy, Michael noted he had previously asked MoD about the devices and data, but received no reply. Ignoring Mr Pleeth's claim, the Coroner told him she wanted to know: *What data was extracted, if it was available to the court, had it been considered, and if not why not?*

The following morning, as the first matter of business, the Coroner sought MoD's reply. Mr Pleeth now gave a very different story:

'The Defence Safety Authority (DSA) is in possession of the GoPro. It was examined, although not directly by the Panel. It shows the transit from RAF Scampton to RAF Valley. It does not show anything of the incident [sic] sortie, and it was relied upon by the DSA to <u>demonstrate serviceability of instruments</u> on the transit. That is the extent they relied upon it, and it is still in the possession of the DSA. As to the mobile phone, there are no records and no-one has any recollection of that ever coming into the possession of the DSA; and so the assumption is it had been seized by the civilian police'.

The Coroner assured Michael her office would make inquiries. It was swiftly determined North Wales Police held the phone. It was returned, and its data extracted by the family. The GoPro, but not its memory card, was returned in February 2022. Michael had to ask again, and was eventually given the card in mid-April.

*

Even in military accidents, the civil police have primacy. If the accident involves a fatality they have a legal responsibility to the Coroner to maintain full control of the crash site, until the deceased have been located and removed. The site guard is provided by MoD, and its Post Crash Management Incident Officer is responsible for all military activities - but must comply with police instructions. North Wales Police relinquished primacy to him the following day. His report is listed as an Exhibit in the Panel's report, but has not been released.

The first task, the golden rule of accident investigation, is to secure the wreckage. As no police report or interviews have been released, and no police witnesses appeared, this aspect of the investigation remains an unknown; an entirely unsatisfactory situation. But given the police removed the phone, they either (a) also removed the GoPro and later returned it to MoD, or (b) by agreement they 'allowed' MoD to retain it. Upon its return to the family, forensic examination revealed it was accessed on 22 and 26 March 2018. It contains just under 12 minutes of video from the outbound flight from RAF Scampton. The nature of GoPros is that they can record High and Low definition versions of each video, and this was the case here. The device recorded external audio, not intercom. There were of over 300 unrecoverable files, meaning they had been deleted and/or overwritten; but it cannot be known when.

Had the devices been returned and Mr Pleeth simply said *'No data was recorded of the accident flight'*, this aspect would barely warrant a mention. MoD <u>must</u> know this. The lie, and withholding the camera for a further three months, is dubious behaviour. Was there something to conceal?

The instruments referred to were the Jon's Barometric Altimeters, the video revealing what the pressure settings were during the outward leg. However, that does not prove serviceability. It is like saying *I filled my car up with petrol, therefore it will pass its MoT*.

Figure 7 is a screenshot of video recorded by Jon at 0944, 20 minutes out from Scampton. At top right, the Standby Altimeter. This continues to operate even with the loss of both Inverters (providing AC power). At bottom left, the Main Altimeter repeater, replicating the pilot's. While the front is slaved to the rear, the barometric reference is not, so Flight Lieutenant Stark had to advise Jon what to set them to before leaving Scampton; and what to change them to as and when required. 1028 hectopascals (or millibars) is shown, which the Panel said was correct for this point in the flight. (Three minutes earlier it was 1013). The instruments are only shown on a few fleeting frames of video.

Figure 7 - XX204 Rear cockpit Barometric Altimeters.

The apparent error of ~80 feet between the two instruments is entirely normal and noted in the Aircrew Manual - a natural lag caused by their different designs. A good rule of thumb is that the allowable error in a Pitot Static instrument is the width of the pointer. Such instruments can be remarkably accurate if calibrated correctly, but manoeuvring can cause ram air to momentarily enter the static ports, forcing inaccuracies; although the Hawk system is quite resistant to this. It can be seen from the Attitude Indicator (top left) that the aircraft is in a slightly descending right bank, which would have little if any effect.

However, the Panel noted abnormalities in the Altitude Transducer - a separate instrument (using the same air source) sending data to the

Accident Data Recorder. These included: indicating runway height after take-off, a period of constant indicated altitude at the apex of the PEFATO profile, and a discontinuity of data after the start of the final turn. These manifested when a rate of change of height commenced, and were caused by a 'sticky' transducer (the Panel did not elaborate); which is an unserviceability but impossible to pick up in-flight. (Data is downloaded for analysis every 75 flying hours, at which point the fault would be identified). Consequently, the Panel had difficulty reconstructing the height profile of the flight and, in my opinion, came to fair conclusions. Nevertheless, the aircraft's altitude cannot be known accurately at any point in the flight between take-off and impact.

Under pressure

Prior to 1983, MoD used the ubiquitous Smiths Industries Pitot Static Test Set. When tuning or testing such an instrument, from zero to full scale and back, one would manually turn a valve, replicating the gradual change in pressure when changing altitude. A sticky capsule (aneroid barometer) or movement (electro-mechanical or mechanical linkage) would be immediately evident. However, a new type 'digital' test set was procured on which one set an upper and lower pressure (altitude), pressed a button and the pressure would change more or less instantaneously. The obvious problem is that in real life an aircraft does not behave in this way. If the fragile capsules survived the violent change in pressure, any stickiness would not manifest. Worse, their mechanical properties might change, making calibration almost impossible and the most expensive component having to be replaced more often.

Another effect was the sudden jolt would make the quadrant jump off the hand staff pinion, and the pointer would fall back to below zero and stay there. In practice, a repaired instrument is tested at the air station before fitting - which would often cause the above. The same instrument might be returned for repair 3 or 4 times a year without having been near an aircraft. The waste was astronomical.

No longer having the correct test equipment, Andy Speedie, an MoD instrument fitter, developed a simple modification to prevent this in Lynx Airspeed Indicators - over-sized nylon washers either side of the pinion. The trouble was, he modified over 300 before telling anyone! His reply was 'Check the serial numbers - not one of them has come back for repair'. No arguing with that, Andy.

112

My point is this. Andy and his colleagues had met their obligation by reporting the test set was not fit for purpose. They'd been ignored. There are many similar examples even in the two main cases discussed here - Sean Cunningham and Jon - of maintainers forced to make the best of a bad job. Ultimately, what he did was not strictly correct (an understatement), but I would never criticise *him*. A quiet word was sufficient. MoD did not 'de-modify' any of the instruments; but nor did it formally adopt the modification. That was far worse.

Release to Service compliance

Every item of equipment that forms part of the aircraft, or if carried even if not used, must have a level of clearance; and that must be stated in the Release to Service. Lacking this, the equipment is not permitted in the aircraft. These clearance levels are:

- Installation Only
- Switch-On Only *(Can be used, but not to be relied upon in any way).*
- Limited
- Full

Equipment Not Basic to the Air System, including Carry-On Equipment such as laptops and cameras, must also be listed in the Release; and to ensure they are correctly identified and understood Safety Assessments are required. These rules are sacrosanct. They exist for the safety of the aircraft, its occupants, groundcrew, and those whom it overflies.

But groundcrew don't work to the Release. They work to Group and Local Orders. Jon was carrying a GoPro Hero 5, which was not listed. So, what persuaded him this was permitted? The Red Arrows Display Directive, which Circus *would* heed, states:

'Circus engineers are not to use cameras in the cockpit without the permission of the pilot. Cameras should not be used at critical stages of flight such as take-off and landing'.

To Jon, this was his permission. *Just ask the pilot if it's okay.* But the Display Directive should have reflected the Release to Service - *The use of hand-held cameras is not permitted.* If (say) 22 Group thought their use of potential benefit, then it should have initiated the clearance process. Once again the Directive, issued by the Delivery Duty Holder (Commandant Central Flying School), and endorsed by the Operating Duty Holder (AOC 22 Group), cannot be reconciled with the Aircraft

Document Set.

Generically, the main risk is Electro-Magnetic Interference, particularly with navigation, fuel and control systems. Also, it is a loose article hazard and if dropped may interfere with the ejection seat mechanism or controls. Self-evidently, these are potentially critical threats.

*

What of aircraft equipment? This is where things get interesting.

The Hawk T.1/1A Release to Service, of March 2022, permits a Mounted GoPro Camera System to be fitted under Service Modification 214. (That is, its safety is underwritten by MoD). This upgrades the system from a GoPro Hero 2, to Hero 6 or 7, and retains severe Limitations:

- *'In-cockpit charging of GoPro video equipment is prohibited'.*

- *'In-cockpit GoPro video equipment must have WIRELESS CONNECTIONS selected to OFF when on or near the aircraft'.*

And of greater import is a WARNING (indicating *'the consequence of not respecting a Limitation might be death and/or injury'*):

'Electro-Magnetic Interference from in-cockpit GoPro video equipment could interfere with Safety Critical Systems, even with WIRELESS CONNECTIONS selected to OFF'. (MoD's emphasis).

Was this briefed to Circus members before flying? And, plainly, it is vital that all evidence from the scene is preserved; and not manhandled by (e.g.) local police who, regardless of their primacy, would seldom understand these issues and certainly not have a copy of the Release to Service. The device was accessed two and six days after the accident, but was a record kept of the wireless connection setting?

Moreover, the Red Arrows Risk Register included RED/LOCI-HAN/05 'Use of hand-held cameras', raised on 22 May 2008:

'Selected photographers allowed to use cameras during taxi, take-off and landing, contrary to Training Group Orders'.

'Contrary to' is clearly an expression of concern. The Delivery Duty Holder ruled:

'Limited approval given to experienced aviation photographers, and only with the pilot's consent and appropriate safety briefing. Cameras required to have wrist strap, long neck straps to be removed before flight'.

But this is not a blanket approval. The obvious questions are:

- Did the Duty Holder realise he was contradicting the mandated Release to Service?

- Are any engineers, in addition to the Circus photographer, certified, and what constitutes *'experienced'*? Has the Commandant delegated the authority to issue these certifications? Indeed, does he hold such authority, given he is contradicting the Release to Service?

- Were Circus engineers made aware of the Limitations, Warnings, and potential effect on (unspecified) Safety Critical Systems?

- As the effect on Safety Critical Systems was unknown (*'could interfere with'*), what persuaded Duty Holders to place the Air System at an unquantified risk?

The Panel did not ignore this entirely. It asked one pilot:

"Do you know if the cameras need to be cleared in the Release to Service?'

'I do not know the answer to that question'.

The correct answer is *'Yes, they do'*, and all pilots should know this. They need to know what is in the Release, and sign to say they do; but they must also know what is *meant* to be in it. The Panel did not explore this further, which is a major omission and probably directed. Of note, the US Marine Corps (for example) prohibit the use of such devices *'on grounds that they can incentivise risk-taking and serve as a distraction'.*

There are many other areas of uncertainty, such as *'the fitness for purpose of the Personal Locator Beacons post-ejection is unknown'.* But pilots want, need, to be assured that any emergency equipment has been tested and trialled before acceptance. The Release is meant to provide that assurance. It is the Master Airworthiness Reference. The title tells you that it <u>must</u> be right. Perhaps more fundamentally, any comment about fitness for purpose - an operational term - has no place in the Release, and is indicative of serious systemic failures. (Because the same department is responsible for all RAF Releases to Service).

*

Suffice to say, the Panel would have been wise to construct a compliance matrix to illustrate breaches. And explain why the Release now seems to incorporate an abbreviated Constraints Document, which in its proper form articulates Operational Constraints and Limitations, and hence expenditure priorities for each platform. Whereas, the Release must reflect UK policy to operate a Limitations-based airworthiness system.

However, it at least reveals concerns and tries to deal with them. But 22

115

Group, Central Flying School and the Red Arrows management seemingly ignored its mandate, inviting accusations of acting as a law unto themselves. Of course, it is equally possible they have a letter from the Chief of the Air Staff overruling his subordinate, saying *It's okay for everyone to use any camera*. But I doubt it. Either way, the Military Aviation Authority should be invited to comment on why they remain content their mandates are viewed as optional.

I do not suggest these breaches relating to the GoPro and phone caused or contributed to the accident or death. But I do state, categorically, that it is further evidence of wider systemic failings which certainly did.

Recurrence

MoD has form here. In the aftermath of the 1994 Mull of Kintyre accident (Chinook ZD576), all personal electronic devices (phones, laptops, pagers, personal digital assistants) were spirited away by the police and Security Services. Yet, potentially, they contained crucial evidence as to the accident timeline, without which it was guesswork. That guesswork was then used to condemn the pilots.

MoD claimed the devices (thought to be around 30, plus watches) had all been examined and eliminated as the source of Electro-Magnetic Interference. In fact, 15 years later it emerged that only two generic mobile phones (i.e. not from the wreckage) had been tested. To every Inquiry MoD implied they were from the accident.

Caught out, the RAF claimed the devices had never been in MoD's possession. The evidence of the Senior Air Accidents Investigation Branch Inspector, Mr Tony Cable, emphatically refuted this. The devices had been collected before his arrival at the scene. (MoD will not say by whom). He saw them laid out on a table, but was prevented from examining them. The President of the Board, later Chief of the Air Staff, knew they had been removed, denying Mr Cable vital evidence.

Subsequently, and as of 2022, MoD, the Crown Office and Police Scotland have refused to act on this fresh evidence of gross misconduct, failure to disclose evidence, and mishandling of physical evidence. Those responsible will not discuss the matter, and have refused to return the devices to families. Given this behavioural trend, one is entitled to be sceptical about MoD's current claims and motives.

Selective complicity

Who would be expected to know the detail of these systemic failings?

The pilot's solicitors knew, as they had contacted me on 13 March 2020 seeking advice on increased weight of the aircraft over the years, the effect on handling, and whether the Aircraft Document Set reflected this. Also, any issues I knew of that had been omitted by the Service Inquiry.[70] They confirmed to me they were concentrating on MoD's systemic failings. While I naturally gravitate towards assisting the bereaved, I knew the correspondent from previous cases (Hawk XX177 and the Sea King mid-air, where she represented the families). I copied her with my letter to the Coroner of 17 October 2019, in which I had notified him of common factors between XX177 (2011) and XX204. I also sent it to the family solicitors, offering my assistance.[71] They replied on 17 April 2020, declining.[72] When I later spoke to the family, I learned they were unaware of my offer.

The Coroner knew, because both she and her predecessor had been advised in October 2019, and on a number of subsequent occasions. MoD's QC, Mr Pleeth? Perhaps not the detail, and MoD would never tell him - although he was clearly warned to avoid certain subjects, such as risk, airworthiness and prior occurrences.

As the family was excluded from legal discussions, it cannot be known what was said between these other parties. But, tellingly, Mr Pleeth's claim at the Pre-Inquest Hearing in 2021, that there had been no systemic failings, came as no surprise to the Coroner.

What of North Wales Police? They conducted no investigation and were not in court, yet were found years later to be in possession of physical evidence from the scene. Should they not have declared this to the Coroner? Did their seizure, handling and retention of evidence comply with the Police and Criminal Evidence Act? Did they examine it without the Panel present? It has not been demonstrated that the chain of custody remains unbroken. These are very serious matters, and elsewhere would be sufficient to declare a mistrial or quash a conviction.

*

When directed to meet a legal obligation, and shown the procedures to

---

70 E-mail Irwin Mitchell LLP/Hill, 13 March 2020 16:55.
71 E-mail Hill/Bolt Burdon Kemp LLP, 18 March 2020 17:01.
72 E-mail Bolt Burdon Kemp/Hill, 17 April 2020 12:47.

be followed, people with formal delegation don't just make an accidental decision to ignore them. They either meet their obligation (which includes saying if they don't know how, or don't want to), or wilfully don't. In the first instance that may be simple disobedience or abrogation. But when accompanied by a written declaration that the directive *has* been implemented, that is subject to two years imprisonment under the Armed Forces Act. The offenders are known, because their signatures are appended. But unless they speak up, it cannot be known if they were directed to make their false declarations.

Was MoD allowed to make private submissions, persuading the Coroner not to go there? Henceforth, with the one exception (the question on stall warning, and even then she allowed MoD to refuse to answer), she was intolerant of any questions that sought to establish why the failures had been allowed to occur, and why they had been condoned at the highest levels of the RAF, MoD and government. Most obviously, she did not address evidence of systemic failings which she knew had been accepted by other Coroners and had formed the basis of the Nimrod Review. MoD led her to believe the failures were applicable only to the accident aircraft, on that one day.

Nevertheless, this is the first time a Coroner has ruled that breaches occurred and linked them directly to other accidents; meaning Ms Sutherland accepted them as systemic. But she did not spell this out. She did not say to Mr Pleeth *'You are wrong about systemic failings'*, or *'You did not tell the truth over the GoPro and phone'*; far less sanction him. If any witness had made such claims, that would be perjury; but it is seemingly acceptable for MoD to mislead its legal team, knowing they will in turn mislead the court. She did not comment on the contradictions in MoD's evidence, or the defensive and evasive demeanour of some witnesses. Charged with establishing cause of *death*, she instead allowed herself to be steered towards two factors in the cause of the *accident*. Asked by the family why she acquiesced, she would not say; nor discuss the basis upon which she agreed there were serious systemic failings, and then refused to allow questions on them.

I conclude that the scope of the Inquest was carefully bounded in MoD's favour. The family's presence in court was the system going through the motions. The Inquest has been closed, but it has not been completed.

The Coroner's Decision

Ms Sutherland adjourned the Inquest *'part-heard'*, stating this would give her time to consider a 'Prevention of Future Deaths Report' (or Regulation 28 report) to the Secretary of State for Defence. But first, the family would have to wait for her written decision, which she said would be issued on 3 December 2021. On that day she read it to the camera in a largely empty courthouse. She confirmed her report would be restricted to two matters of concern, relating to lack of simulator training and stall warner. Cause of death was to be ignored.

Ms Sutherland decided that a charge of gross negligence manslaughter against the pilot was inappropriate, but did not consider the offences committed by other individuals. Nor the breaches that actually caused Jon's death. She did, however, agree that the corporate MoD had been negligent; but not to a gross degree. That, the breaches *'did not fall far below what can reasonably be expected of the organisation in the circumstances'*. Also, *'there was not a sufficiency of evidence'* of these breaches; despite them being set out in MoD's reports and explained to her in written submissions. But in a way she was correct, as she had not allowed the evidence to be heard in court. Judicial and actual truth again.

*

To avoid duplication, I will restrict myself to a brief analysis of elements not previously discussed:

> *'(Regarding) fitment of an artificial stall warning capability, upon request by me Group Captain Jackson provided a further Statement after the conclusion of his oral evidence. Following a non-fatal Hawk T.1 air crash in* 2010 *where the cause of the crash was due to a stall, that resulted from an approach flown below the promulgated minimum speeds, a recommendation was made by the Board of Inquiry to investigate the fitment of an audio stall warning system. The decision made was to close that recommendation without actioning due to other mitigating factors being deemed appropriate at that time'.*

The accident referred to occurred on 20 April 2007 to Hawk T.1 XX196 at RAF Mona on Anglesey, where the pilot stalled and ejected safely. MoD has not released any report. 2010 is when a feasibility study into a stall warner was completed, and a Cost Benefit Analysis took until July 2012. In May 2014 a decision was made not to proceed. Over seven years from accident to decision... Why did the Coroner not ask the question of someone who knew of crashes further back than 2007; or indeed crashes with the same cause of death? And why only mention a stall warner when front seat Command Eject - the lack of which was a root cause of Jon's death - had also been rejected?

(There *was* a Red Arrows accident in 2010, a mid-air collision between XX233 and XX253 over Crete. The main causal factor was failure to maintain minimum safe distance. The injured pilot, thankfully fully recovered, replaced Flight Lieutenant Stark in 2018).

'The Defence Safety Authority (DSA), whilst independent from the RAF and indeed a single service authority, is an agency in the Ministry of Defence and reports to the Secretary of State for Defence. The DSA is therefore the investigating authority within the very department of State which may be held responsible for any breaches found. This position contrasts with the civilian context of the legislative framework granting investigatory powers into accidents in flight to the Civil Aviation Authority only and not to the Health and Safety Executive.

The court is under an Article 2 duty to investigate which is not the same duty placed on the Ministry of Defence. The DSA investigation is not necessarily capable on its own of constituting a Coroner's compliance with the Article 2 obligation. Such an investigation absent the Coroner, also lacks involvement of the family and would unlikely meet the requirements of Article 2 or be a meaningful Inquest for the family. The court must fulfil its Article 2 procedural requirement by including relevant matters in its public decision/summing up and also its Conclusion.

Importantly, the MoD also had the opportunity to ask relevant questions of MoD witnesses. The MoD suggests that anything not covered in the report that forms the basis of the court's public reasoning and conclusion would be speculative and thus unlawful. Such a restrictive approach would limit the Inquest to assess the evidence in a vacuum and reduce the court's role to a rubber-stamping exercise of a report submitted by the MoD. The court is obliged to consider the live evidence and make determinations on relevant issues. Therefore, where they are not a duplication or technical in nature, they fall to be determined by the court. I accept the vast majority of the findings and adopt those as my own. I say the vast majority as I make different findings in some respects which I reach by weighing up the evidence in the Service Inquiry Report with the evidence that I have heard'.

Significantly, the Coroner states that the DSA/MAA is not independent of MoD, only of the RAF (itself arguable given its predominantly RAF make-up). Another first. MoD simply ignored her.

*

120

The following day, 4 December 2021, I wrote again to Ms Sutherland:

'Your confirmation that risks were not ALARP has particular resonance. By definition, therefore, and in addition to having no Safety Case, the aircraft was flying under an invalid Master Airworthiness Reference. This repeats a root cause of many accidents. For example Chinook ZD576 (29 killed), Nimrod XV230 (14), C-130 XV179 (10), Hawk XX177 (1), Sea Kings XV650 & 704 (7), Chinook ZA710 (7), Tornado ZG710 (2); and more.

Therefore, at what point, or at what number of deaths, does the same failure become gross? It is a fair question, because in each case the deaths would have been prevented by the simple application of mandated regulations - and in each case a false declaration was made that they had been implemented. In my opinion, these repeated failures are so reprehensible, and fall so far below the standards expected, they are criminal. "Manslaughter" is generous. The impact on the bereaved is no less than that of murder'.

Receiving no reply, and after speaking to Michael and Gayle, I wrote again on 7 December 2021 on their behalf:

'You raise two matters of concern relating to lack of (1) a warning system, and (2) representative training. These are known systemic failings, and have killed many. They can be summarised - flat refusal to implement mandated airworthiness regulations.

Also, cause of accident and cause of death have been conflated. The two matters of concern relate to the former. That death was avoidable is plain. Flight Lieutenant Stark survived. The real question of concern must be why didn't Jonathan Bayliss. What actually caused his death? In the first instance, it was him being left behind in the aircraft. The known hazard and associated risk were noted in the Red Arrows Risk Register, but it was deemed sufficient that the pilot survive. The Command Eject system was not fit for the purpose to which the aircraft was being put. Jonathan was formally declared expendable.

In addition to making the Hawk airworthy, the action required of MoD was to (a) cease flying such passengers, or (b) fit a suitable Command Eject system. It recklessly decided to do neither, while making a false declaration that the risks were Tolerable and ALARP. This repeats the same offences (under the Armed Forces and Air Force Acts) committed in over 70 deaths notified to you. For brevity I have omitted many more. Where is the accountability for these blatantly illegal actions?'

No reply.

*

The family issued a statement:

'MoD has been able to get away with too much in the past. By making this an Article 2 Inquest its systemic failings were front and centre. It has breached its duty to protect the life of a serviceman in its employment. Unbeknown to Jon, he assumed a huge amount of risk on 20 March 2018, risk that should have mitigated by Duty Holders to Tolerable and As Low As Reasonably Practicable. The Inquest highlights repetitive problems from past accidents, ignored recommendations from past fatality reports, and denied funding to the squadron that resulted in vastly undermanned and underfunded conditions.

The family are pleased that many of the recommendations have been implemented, but have concern that the modification to the command ejection system is still outstanding. If the pilot had had the ability to eject the rear seat, Jon would still be with us today. In the family's view the jets are flying unsafely until the stall warning is fitted, and rear seat personnel are at risk from unforeseen emergencies until the system is modified. To the best of our knowledge there has never been an Air System Safety Case produced for the Hawk T.1 for its current use. Without this the aircraft should not be flying.

Institutions like the MoD have a duty to protect the life of our servicemen and women, therefore scrutiny and pressure from society and media should be relentless to achieve this goal'.

Ms Sutherland wrote to me on 7 December confirming her decision was a public document, meaning I was permitted to discuss it. Had the media or public wanted a copy before official publication they had to submit a formal request in writing. This effectively prevented adverse reporting, and there has been no coverage of the decision.

Regulation 28 Report - The Coroner's Matters of Concern

Two versions of the report were released. First to Secretary of State for Defence Ben Wallace MP, and three days later to the family. The public version had various names and, inexplicably, the aircraft tail number, redacted. The family were given an unredacted version. Ms Sutherland listed two matters of concern:

'As identified by the Service Inquiry the cause of death was the aircraft stalling with insufficient height to recover. It was also recognised that the aircraft may in certain circumstances stall without pre-stall buffet. The pre-stall buffet remains the warning sign to the pilot of an impending stall. The Service Inquiry recommended that urgent investigations be undertaken into the incorporation of an artificial stall warning to pilots during low speed low

altitude manoeuvring. Whilst a feasibility assessment and cost benefit analysis have been undertaken a final decision is yet to be made as to whether or not the recommendations will be adopted. The current out of service date for the said aircraft is at least 2030. A number of RAF Aerobatic Team pilots will be flying every year (including a small number of new arrivals each year) and some circus engineers are still being flown in the said aircraft.

It was recommended by the Service Inquiry that the Hawk T.1/1A simulator training accurately reflects an aerodynamic model of a RAF aerobatic aircraft with smoke pod fitted, given that this may soon become the only Hawk T.1/1A operated by the RAF and the current training simulator did not have the effect of a smoke pod fitted. Whilst there are developments in this respect there is no new synthetic trainer in place yet.

In my opinion action should be taken to prevent future death and I believe you have the power to take such action. You are under a duty to respond to this report within 56 days of the date of this report, namely 1 February 2022. I, the Coroner, may extend the period. Your response must contain details of action taken or proposed to be taken, setting out the timetable for action. Otherwise, you must explain why no action is proposed'.

While confirming MoD's negligence and failure of duty of care, the Coroner did not say what the breaches were. Readers had no reference point, and were left to infer there were only two, they related to her two matters of concern, and in turn caused death. She omitted all the root causes of death, and that they were recurring. In particular, Command Eject, incorrect Safety Statements, and failure to implement mandates. Had she mentioned any of these, and that they had caused previous deaths, her decision that the admitted breaches were not gross would have been undermined.

A copy was sent to the Chief Coroner, His Honour Judge Thomas Teague QC, who would perhaps realise this repeated the public concerns notified to him on 1 July 2021 - which he had not replied to.

*

Today, the baseline for any investigation or Inquiry into a death arising from a military aircraft accident must be the evidence provided to the Nimrod Review in 2007, after the loss of Nimrod XV230 in September 2006; and upon which Mr Haddon-Cave QC based his primary findings. It then formed the basis of the main submission to the Mull of Kintyre Review; and the XX204 Service Inquiry report is just the latest to confirm its validity. Such an impressive evidential trail is what independent investigators dream of.

But to MoD and legal authorities it is their worst nightmare. The official position remains unchanged. MoD pays lip service to the Reviews, formally rejecting the basis upon which the Military Aviation Authority was formed. (That is, systemic failings). It cannot see the absurdity of this. Upon this premise it engages with Coroners, rendering the Inquest itself an absurdity. Case in point.

The impact on the Sean Cunningham case

In 2018, a member of the accident investigation team was chief witness against Martin-Baker, despite his Military Aviation Authority (MAA) superiors being directly involved in the decision that killed Sean. The potential impact on that prosecution is immense. The basis upon which the Health and Safety Executive (HSE), Crown Prosecution Service and Lincolnshire Police decided not to pursue MoD is now untenable.

The admission in Jon's case, that MoD repeated its failure to disseminate information, makes the HSE's prosecution of Martin-Baker even more unsafe, and gives lie to the claim to the Lincolnshire Coroner that its breaches were being addressed. The company pleaded guilty for commercial reasons, to avoid the case impinging on a major contract they were bidding for. But a guilty plea does not negate the obligation to review new or fresh evidence. Ms Sutherland has, correctly, directly linked the two deaths. Even if Martin-Baker had committed the alleged offence (which they quite definitely did not - the Judge, Dame Justice Carr, listing eight reasons why they were not culpable), there is now formal legal acceptance of greater, systemic failings by MoD. The police and HSE are now obliged to act.

On 26 January 2022 these matters were put to the Lincolnshire Chief Constable, Chris Haward. He was asked to review this fresh evidence, especially in the light of existing written, verbal and video evidence which his predecessor had refused to assess; and consider the *prima facie* evidence of prosecutorial misconduct by the HSE. He replied on 3 February 2022 claiming that, in less than a day, he had thoroughly reviewed the evidence (which included hours of video and hundreds of pages of written submissions) and decided that the HSE should retain primacy. That is, judge its own case. *Truly exceptionally bad?*

10. Prior occurrence

We have seen MoD's default position - there have been no systemic failings, and no recurrence. By refusing to heed mandates it has forced itself into the lie. As families have no prior input to investigations, it is only at the Inquest they can pose questions and assess MoD's reaction. By which time it is too late; especially when the key witness refuses to reply, is last to be heard, and matters are wrapped up minutes after he leaves the stand. Therefore, and unavoidably, much of the evidence in this chapter was uncovered after the Inquest.

MoD's denial of any commonality with the death of Sean Cunningham, despite 12 readily identifiable recurrences set out in its own reports, was so ludicrous one almost felt embarrassed. It was the clue something greater was being concealed. An assessment of past Hawk accidents was necessary. The internet contains details (but not necessarily facts) drawn from official reports; but also relies on the memory of contributors and so cannot, for current purposes, be called evidence. But by comparing this data with MoD's website, which hosts many accident reports, it was clear that others had never been published.

The official way to gain access is to make a Freedom of Information request. The first stumbling block is that MoD broadly ignores the 20-day requirement to provide information (but is by no means the worst in this respect). I have long since given up on some requests; but the refusal to reply speaks volumes and confirms you are on the right path. The delineation is invariably how embarrassing the information will be to MoD; and indeed today this is one of the criteria used when determining security classifications, offering it a further exemption under the Act and negating its intent.

Also, the Information Commissioner (in England and Wales) has ruled that replies need not be truthful, and there is no obligation to correct errors.[73] This applies both to general information and personal data. The most relevant example of this I am aware of is a letter dated 23 April 2003 to the Permanent Under-Secretary of State (provided under Freedom of Information), in which the Defence Procurement Agency made disparaging and frankly libellous claims about the officer who

---

73 Letter, Information Commissioner's Office RFA0169687, 5 October 2007.

reported the systemic airworthiness failings later confirmed by the Nimrod Review, informing the Permanent Under-Secretary of State there was no substance to them. This remains MoD's official position.

Most infamously, in 2010 the Air Staff claimed to Dr Susan Phoenix, whose husband Ian had died in Chinook ZD576, that there was no such thing as a Release to Service. Think about that. A Minister, Sir Nick Harvey MP, was given a letter to sign containing a fabrication so blatant that MoD's most junior staff would recognise it.[74] When given the opportunity by Susan to correct himself, he repeated it.[75] He was then forced to apologise when I provided the Release and his letters to Lord Philip.[76] A reasonable person might expect him to demand the head of the person who wrote the briefs. But no. The apology was meaningless as he continued to support the Air Staff. I relate this event as it is important to understand just what families are up against. And, of course, it is compelling evidence of corporate violations.

Another factor is that MoD has no single archive. For example, RAF accident reports are stored with the Air Historical Branch in Ruislip, NW London. Aircraft engineering records are at RAF Innsworth, Gloucestershire. Project office files are usually at Kew, in SW London. Potentially revealing or embarrassing papers are often destroyed. But only rarely will there be a single copy. At the very least, there will be the originator's and recipient's copies. And staff who make airworthiness decisions are encouraged to retain personal copies, as they may have to be defended. (A good example is the Sea King mid-air of 2003). In the case of the Chinook Release to Service, there were 39 recipients on the distribution list; which highlights both the stupidity of denying its existence, and the extreme anxiety that drove the denial.

Hawk T.1A XX334, RAF Chivenor, 30 September 1992

On 8 November 2021 the Daily Telegraph published a letter from retired Wing Commander Jeremy Parr, setting out his personal experience of this 1992 accident, and MoD's prior knowledge of risk:

'An Inquest has been considering the death of a Red Arrows engineer, Corporal Jonathan Bayliss, at RAF Valley in 2018. My reaction was the pilot was

---

74 Letter MSU/04/07/03/01/cc, 11 May 2010.
75 Letter MSU/4/7/3/2/is, 28 September 2010.
76 Letter MSU/4/7/3/2, 16 June 2011.

practising a "turnback". This manoeuvre is questionable in its efficacy and carries a high risk; the aircraft is on the cusp of the stall throughout and, given the aerodynamics of the Hawk wing, once it goes wrong there is no way out. As Officer Commanding Flying at RAF Chivenor in 1992, I was involved in the Board of Inquiry into an identical accident. Twenty-six years later Corporal Bayliss lost his life, and it could have been avoided'.

Unfortunately this was too late to use at the Inquest, which had finished a few days before on 4 November.

But out of the blue, on 22 January 2022 I received an e-mail from a name familiar to me from the Sean Cunningham case. It simply said 'FYI', and attached a safety report written by Air Commodore Martin Abbott, RAF Director of Flight Safety, on 23 March 1993, following the loss of XX334.[77] These reports were issued separately to the Board of Inquiry report, their purpose being to emphasise safety failings. As Wing Commander Parr stated, the accidents were <u>identical</u>. In both cases the rear seater was unable to react, either in the air or after impact.

An interesting linkage is that six weeks before the accident, on 14 August 1992, Air Commodore Abbott had submitted his Chinook Airworthiness Review Team (CHART) report to Air Marshal Michael Alcock, the RAF Chief Engineer, and Air Vice Marshal Antony Bagnall, Assistant Chief of the Air Staff.[78] (The latter issued the Release to Service that his successors denied the existence of, the former was responsible for ensuring airworthiness regulations were implemented within the RAF). The report had never been circulated, and was only uncovered in 2011. It comprised 373 pages confirming the systemic airworthiness failings in excruciating detail. Many of its recommendations were to be repeated, *ad nauseum*, in subsequent accident reports. With the benefit of hindsight, and other recently uncovered reports, it is clear the Director was thoroughly fed up with Boards of Inquiry being interfered with and directed as to their findings, with systemic failings going unchecked.

MoD's website hosts reports from eight stall-related accidents between 1982 and 2007, killing five pilots and severely injuring others. It does <u>not</u> host these XX334 reports.

As for the Board's report, it is heavily redacted. Every name is concealed,

---

77 D/IFS(RAF)/140/42/92/I 'RAF Aircraft Accident Report Hawk T.1A XX334, 30 September 1992', published 23 March 1993.
78 D/IFS(RAF) 125/30/2/1, 14 August 1992. CHART report.

along with any information that might help identification. The redactions were made post-Freedom of Information Act 2000, evidenced by annotations referring to the Act. However, the pilot being found negligent to a gross degree was *not* redacted, and his name was reported at the time; suggesting a different motive for redacting it many years later. To be in a position to redact the master copy and withhold it from being published narrows matters down; and it is plain to me that the motive was to conceal recurrence.

Summary of accident

The instructor, in the *front* seat, was demonstrating the manoeuvre to Flight Lieutenant Philip Martin, an experienced Qualified Flying Instructor who was undertaking Qualified Weapons Instructor training. Martin had requested that he practice a turnback, and it was decided that the instructor would demonstrate it first. Three other aircraft were lined up behind them, so there was a degree of pressure to complete the manoeuvre successfully.

Shortly after take-off, at 250 knots and 380 feet, the instructor initiated a turnback by setting the engine to idle and turned left through 35°, simultaneously converting speed to height.[79] Whilst climbing he reversed the turn to the right and, at 1230 feet, looking over his shoulder, decided he had sufficient height to make a successful approach, and reduced speed further to 160 knots in order to reduce the radius of turn.

As he turned the aircraft in light buffet towards the runway he was closer to the airfield than he would have preferred. Although not ideally positioned, he still judged he could complete the manoeuvre. Whilst in the right hand turn, at 550 feet he selected landing gear down. While the gear was travelling, he noted the airspeed was below 160 knots, at which point he selected full flap for landing.

At full flap the aircraft was still in a 20° banked right-hand turn at 280 feet, with the airspeed reducing through 147 knots. At 260 feet and 142 knots, heading 55° to 60° off runway heading, he reversed the turn to regain the runway centre-line. He was now aware of airframe buffet and

---

79 The instructor challenged this 380 feet, stating he checked the height before commencing the manoeuvre and his instruments read 500 feet. No minimum height was laid down.

observers noted a marked increase in Rate of Descent. At 160 feet and 128 knots, much slower than the recommended speed, he realised he would be unable to complete the manoeuvre. He selected full power and rolled to wings level. Sensing that he would land short, he attempted to cushion the impact by pulling the stick fully back. The nose of the aircraft rose, but realising that the impact would be severe he ejected unannounced. The aircraft struck the ground with wings level, 70m short of the threshold, caught fire as it slid across the ground, hitting a lowered barrier stanchion and finally snagging the barrier net.

The front-seat ejection system functioned correctly, the instructor spending no more than a second under a fully developed canopy before landing heavily on the runway. Flight Lieutenant Martin did not eject.

The crash crew went directly to the burning aircraft and applied foam. After a number of attempts to penetrate the flames they were able to operate the rear canopy Miniature Detonating Cord. Knowing the aircraft was laden with munitions, and despite helmet and boots providing poor protection, and being forced to remove fire resistant gauntlets, in an act of astonishing bravery Senior Aircraftsman Carl Austin (only 20 at the time, and later Lord Mayor of Manchester) climbed on top of the aircraft and with the help of his colleagues pulled Flight Lieutenant Martin out. He was taken immediately to a local hospital by helicopter, but tragically died from severe burns.

The Board of Inquiry commended the *selfless and courageous determination* of the fire crews, and recommended bravery awards. Carl was awarded the Royal Humane Society's Bronze Award, and later a Commander in Chief's Commendation in the Queen's Birthday Honours.

*

It could not be determined why Flight Lieutenant Martin did not eject. Recordings revealed he had only recognised his predicament fractionally before the instructor ejected. Even then, it was uncertain if his expletive was in reaction to unfolding events, or because the fully back control column hindered access to the Seat Pan Firing Handle - a known hazard I mentioned earlier.

It was also considered likely that the security he felt with his instructor's ability may have subdued his awareness of danger. Rendered unconscious by impact (confirmed by the fire crew, who initially thought him dead), he could not eject on the ground. (The ejection seat is a zero-zero design, meaning it works when the aircraft is stationary).

The Board determined that the accident was caused by misjudging the manoeuvre, and not taking standard stall recovery action in sufficient time. It opined that the instructor had the necessary knowledge and skill but did not utilise it, so was negligent. Moreover, by failing to recognise, at the 300 feet point, that successful completion of his final turn onto runway heading was impossible, he was negligent to a gross degree. He was 'reproofed', or reprimanded, by the Air Officer Commanding-in-Chief Support Command, Air Chief Marshal Sir John Willis.

*

Crucially, the Board made two related recommendations:

1. *'There be a review of the policy on the selection of command ejection detailed at RAF Chivenor Flying Order Book'.*

2. *'The feasibility of providing a command ejection facility from front to rear be examined'.*

On 11 January 1993, Air Officer Commanding Training Units, Air Vice-Marshal (later Air Marshal Sir) Christopher Coville, reviewed these recommendations and directed:

- *'I am content that the RAF Support Command policy, in the form of a Command sponsored Flying Order (which appears in the Chivenor Flying Order Book), is clear and can be adapted to cover all circumstances. I do not, therefore, support a review of policy'.*

- *'Since a relatively high proportion of RAF Support Command Hawk sorties are flown with non-qualified aircrew in the rear seat, the provision of a command eject facility from front to rear is worth pursuing. My staff will approach the Support Authority to task BAe with providing a costed proposal'.*[80]

There are two key issues - the Command Eject recommendation, and an experienced pilot not recognising the situation. Had either been noted in the XX204 report, its wording would have had to be very different. So too the Inquest proceedings. Not least, because front seat Command Eject would have saved Jon.

---

80 Annex A to Part 4 of XX334 Board of Inquiry report 'Remarks of Air Officer Commanding'.

Why was XX334 concealed?

I spoke to Gayle. On the same day I received the report, 22 January 2022, she submitted a Freedom of Information request to the Air Staff:

1. When was front seat command eject, or a feasibility study into it, first recommended by a Board of Inquiry or Service Inquiry?

2. If such recommendations have been made before, by any means, why were they rejected, and by whom?

3. List by date and tail number any Hawk fatal accidents that have occurred whereby the deceased was in the rear seat and not ejected.

They replied on 24 February:

'I can confirm that records as far back as 1979 have been referenced and <u>there is no record of any recommendation or feasibility study before those generated because of the XX204 accident</u>. I can confirm one other instance of a fatal Hawk accident whereby the deceased was in the rear seat and not ejected, which is that of XX334 at RAF Chivenor dated 30 September 1992'.[81]

In other words, they knew of XX334 but denied the content of the report (which they would assume Gayle didn't have). On 17 March 2022 she offered them the opportunity to retract, asking them to *'review the response for accuracy, and update as necessary'*.

The Air Staff Secretariat replied on 14 April 2022:

'I can confirm that following the response to FOI2022/01069, a copy of the full accident report into aircraft XX334 has been found by the Department, dated 30 September 1992. I can confirm that this report made a recommendation for a feasibility study into Front to Rear Command Eject. The Air Officer Commanding in post at that time made the decision <u>not to conduct a study</u> on the basis that the policy covering Command Eject was adequate'.[82]

This conflates the two recommendations, omitting that Air Vice Marshal Coville directed that a feasibility study be conducted; even naming the department that was to initiate the task.

Of particular import, the Coroner had been required to consider the question of gross negligence. One of the major criteria she had been led to believe was not met - recurrence - was now admitted.

One of two things occurred. The initial directive was overruled, or the

---

81 Air Secretariat letter FOI2022/01069, 24 February 2022.
82 Air Secretariat letter FOI2022/01069, 14 April 2022.

study was concluded and the modification rejected. The evidence (from recipients of Air Commodore Abbott's report) suggests the latter. Either way, a record of the decisions must be retained.

*

I revisited the XX204 witness statements. Hitherto unremarkable comments now assumed greater meaning, especially the evidence of Group Captain John Monahan, Commandant Central Flying School and Delivery Duty Holder. He was interviewed on 13 June 2018:

'Has any work been done to consider a Command Eject system that can be initiated from the front?'

'No'.

'Okay'.

'Not that I'm aware of'.

Should he have been? He was undergoing flying training in 1992, and as a junior officer would not necessarily be aware of recommendations. However, in his current capacity he had approved the Safety Statement, and it is inconceivable that in the three months since the accident his staff did not brief him.

Did the Panel try to seek out someone who *was* aware? For example, the Inspectorate of Flight Safety or the Hawk Type Airworthiness Authority? **Or the Hawk staff, including pilots, who visited Martin-Baker's Human Engineering Department in early 2011 seeking details to support their latest bid for front seat Command Eject?**

Their replies would have been very different. It is clear therefore that the requirement was not just forgotten about between 1992 and 2018. It was raised a number of times; and it was incumbent upon the Panel to fill in this timeline, and explain the decisions to reject the modification.

What prompted the question by the Panel? Did it know of XX334, or other instances? And having asked, why did it not explore the issue with the Operating Duty Holder, Air Vice Marshal Warren James, who was interviewed two weeks later on 28 June 2018? In isolation, this might seem a minor oversight. But now the Air Staff have denied the content of the report, it assumes greater, in fact critical, import. The Service Inquiry should be reconvened to interview the decision-makers.

*

Moreover, a number of points raised by the XX334 Board came up again

132

in 2018, among them:

- The Central Flying School should re-examine advice on turnbacks for all aircraft types; and consider ceasing them altogether.

- In 1992 a firm statement was made that Hawk pilots must comply with the Aircrew Manual. But in 2018 key data was only available in FTP3225H.

- At heavy weights, no PEFATO should be initiated below 270 knots. But the Aircraft Document Set did not evolve with the weight of the aircraft, and by 2018 there was a 400kg discrepancy.

- The important differences between a T.1 and 1A were understood in 1992, but considered irrelevant by the XX204 Panel.

- In 1992 the Aircraft Document Set and AP3225H could be reconciled. In 2018 they could not.

Key questions arise:

1. What was the outcome of the 1993 feasibility study, and were there any before or after this?

2. Why was the modification eventually rejected?

3. What was the outcome of the visit to Martin-Baker in 2011?

These are serious issues. The Service Inquiry President stated in court that Jon would be alive had the modification been embodied, so are directly related to the aim of the Inquest. The integrity of both it and the accident investigation has been compromised - and quite deliberately. This is not about blame, or whether the 1992/2011 decisions were right or wrong. It is about the timeframe wherein MoD knew of the risk to life, all the while implying, and later stating under oath, it did not know. *Truly exceptionally bad?*

Other examples

On 1 July 1993, Hawk T.1A XX163 was undertaking a PEFATO at RAF Valley when the aircraft descended rapidly. Despite attempts to apply full power, the instructor took control too late and the aircraft struck the runway hard, causing the undercarriage to collapse. Both crew ejected safely when the aircraft caught fire.

On 20 April 2007, Hawk T.1A XX196 crashed onto the airfield at RAF Mona, Anglesey shortly after take-off from nearby RAF Valley. The solo student pilot had stalled on an overshoot, ejecting safely. The Coroner referred to this accident, citing known risks that were not ALARP.

Another case involved Hawk T.1 XX305 on 28 July 1982 at RAF Valley. This was more complex, the student suffering from smoke inhalation due to a Cold Air Unit failure. The instructor in the rear took over, but was distracted by his concern for the student, whose emergency oxygen supply had run out, and stalled the aircraft in his haste to land. He ejected both of them at 300 feet, but the stall had rolled the aircraft toward the limits of the seat envelope. The instructor survived, although with serious injuries. However, the pilot's seat, firing a split second later, was by now beyond its limits. He had not separated from it when he hit the ground.

As a final example, and as mentioned earlier, Hawk T.1 XX233 was involved in a mid-air collision while practicing with another Red Arrows aircraft, T.1A XX253, in Crete on 20 March 2010. XX233 was written off and the pilot severely injured. XX253 landed safely. The Service Inquiry made a number of familiar comments. Simulator training was inadequate. Aircraft documentation was fragmented. Most relevant was the approach to Risk Management. While a Register was held, it was not subject to review. The remarks of the Convening Authority, Air Vice Marshal Mark Green, Air Officer Commanding 22 Group, were illuminating. He confirmed that *'over the last few years (Risk Management) had become a more formal documented process that is auditable'*, directing that such work be *'undertaken and completed prior to work-up for the 2011 display season'*. He was talking of a routine, mandated process. Elsewhere in MoD the major role of his (2-Star) counterparts was to conduct monthly reviews of the top 10 risks. These reviews form part of the audit trail to 'Tolerable and ALARP' statements, without which the validity of the statement quickly erodes. Green's statement was, in fact, a damning indictment of the continuing failure to implement mandates.

*

The XX204 Service Inquiry Report does not mention these or other similar accidents, despite the requirement to prevent recurrence; and hence does not mention that XX204 was itself a recurrence. Unfortunately the damage was done when MoD's proposed witness list was agreed. The lesson to be learned, and which bears repeating, is that MoD always lies about the same things. Availability of evidence and airworthiness.

11. True colours revealed

On 1 February 2022 the family wrote again to the Coroner, summarising the worst offences and systemic failings. Of agonising distress was:

'The pilot survived, so it is a reasonable assumption that so too would Jonathan. We cannot understand why this was not a matter of concern to you. Making this worse is the statement that it is sufficient the pilot survives in these circumstances. Also, the unforgiveable error in assuming the worst case scenario is injury to the passenger'.

They cited again the XX334 case of 1992, and that the Board of Inquiry report gave lie to MoD's current claim over a feasibility study. They nailed the main problem facing families:

'We had no input to MoD's Service Inquiry, and no-one sought to explain to us the meaning and implications of the many technical, legal and airmanship terms in the report. Only when the heavily redacted report is made public can a knowledgeable person independently assess it and start gathering and analysing the missing evidence'.

Finishing:

'We believe these breaches of duty and failings, which are now seen to have persisted on Hawk since at least 1992, to be gross, and ask that you reappraise your matters of concern and the question of "grossness" as applied to corporate manslaughter. We would also ask that you refer the case to the Health and Safety Executive and North Wales Police'.

Ms Sutherland replied on 15 February 2022:

'As you are aware, you and your family had Interested Person status as part of the Inquest proceedings and fully took part in the Inquest which was undertaken in public. I ensured that you had the full opportunity to address me, question every witness, give evidence and make submissions, as required. The proceedings before me are concluded'.

In other words, *You had your chance, but didn't raise the issues in court.* The message to the family could not be less subtle.

How could proceedings be concluded when the Regulation 28 report had not been answered by Minister, and accepted by the Coroner, thus fulfilling one of the requirements of the Inquest? And while they were allowed to *'question every witness'*, the Coroner seemingly forgets that she allowed them to refuse to answer, and even interjected to prevent them doing so. Moreover, and clearly, the family couldn't raise the 1992 evidence in court, as the accident, and its direct relationship to XX204, was not disclosed by MoD, nor mentioned when specifically asked about prior occurrences.

Ms Sutherland was saying that the family had to fact-check Group Captain Jackson's evidence and, immediately (because he was the final witness), present their case. MoD had over 3.5 years to prepare *its* case. It <u>must</u> have anticipated the question of prior failings and occurrences. It knew about XX334, and how crucial that it be concealed. It orchestrated a cover-up, and the Coroner was an accessory.

The family replied:

> 'In respect of the Corporate Manslaughter and Corporate Homicide Act 2007 section 2 (45) section c, the Inquest finding was that there was negligence but not gross negligence. With the evidence which was not disclosed/withheld by the MoD of the previous deaths caused in similar circumstances, the number of deaths within the Red Arrows now totalling 3 (since 2011), and the MoD having failed to implement the recommendations of previous Service Inquiries, does this not show GROSS NEGLIGENCE on the part of the MoD, and as such should not a verdict of UNLAWFUL KILLING now be recorded?'.[83]

No reply.

*

It can be seen that the decision to make this an Article 2 Inquest, forced upon the Coroner by the evidence, merely shifted the point at which the truth would be concealed. The family were given no prior warning that MoD's main witness - in fact, from their perspective the only relevant witness, as they were told to address key questions on cause of death to him - would be allowed to refuse to answer questions about events before July 2020.

My impression is that those who stood against the family thought to exploit the fact they were no longer legally represented. But, as I have said, the issues here require a deep understanding of MoD procedures and its pattern of behaviour, and few would have imagined the degree of deceit and abuse of entrusted power. It is fair to say some would probably have challenged the 'pre-July 2020' ruling; but none would

---

83 E-mail from Michael Bayliss, 15 February 2022 17:08.

have come up with the XX334 evidence from 1992.

Minister's reply to the Regulation 28 report

On 7 March 2002, Secretary of State Ben Wallace MP replied to Ms Sutherland:

'I understand that you heard evidence of how changes have been made following the recommendations of the Service Inquiry. These include a review of flying training publications, pilot currency requirements and training objectives for Supernumerary Crew. In addition, key safety enhancements such as the creation of a RAFAT-focused Air Safety Management Team, the development of a Command Ejection capability, and the incorporation of a Cockpit Voice Recorder are already in train.

Addressing the matters of concern, you have raised, I set out below the steps already been taken, and the further action planned.

Matters of Concern 1 *- As you observe, further analysis and evaluation has been carried out after the sad death of Corporal Bayliss. I am pleased to say that this has concluded that the incorporation of a combined ASWS [not stated, but Automatic Stall Warning System] and Angle of Attack (AoA) gauge to enhance stall mitigation is feasible and proportionate. The RAF will now take forward work to fit a combined ASWS and AoA gauge to the remaining RAFAT Hawk T.1 aircraft. This will require significant test and evaluation, which will be a high priority. The exact timelines for test, evaluation, development and embodiment of the combined ASWS/AoA gauge will be determined this year.*

RAFAT pilots are regularly required to practice and demonstrate their competence to complete a forced landing. The potential for airframe buffet to be masked by both the 'smoke pod' and when the landing gear is down has been, and will continue to be, a key focus of Hawk T.1 pilot training, combined with the ability to correctly assess a safe approach. The requirement to practise 'live' forced landings will be constantly reviewed, in-line with the development of a combined ASWS/AoA gauge and as future RAFAT Hawk T.1 synthetic developments are realised.

Continued training and the application of both a combined ASWS and AoA gauge, will collectively aim to ensure pilots are prepared and have sufficient warning during low-speed low-altitude manoeuvring.

Matters of Concern 2 *- The Ministry of Defence (MoD) recognises that the Hawk Synthetic Training Facility at RAF Valley provides a generic platform* *for procedural and emergency training, for pilots that operate all types of Hawk T.1 aircraft. The retirement of the 'black' Hawk T.1, which includes 736 Royal Naval Air Squadron and Number 100 Squadron, on 31 March 2022, provides an opportunity to deliver a bespoke Hawk Synthetic Training Facility for RAFAT pilots. The RAF has begun to identify potential RAFAT focused Hawk Synthetic Training Facility options, to be co-located with the Team at their new home of RAF Waddington. The new Facility will correctly reflect the aerodynamic model of a RAFAT aircraft, with a smoke pod fitted. A detailed procurement timeline is being developed, with the expectation that the new Facility will be in place by 2025.*

Prior to this being completed, it is important that RAFAT pilots can train synthetically on an aircraft that is truly representative of the one they fly. MoD has therefore taken steps to ensure that, following the retirement of the 'black' Hawk T.1 aircraft, the current Hawk Synthetic Training Facility software is updated to closely reflect the aerodynamic model of a RAFAT aircraft with a smoke pod fitted. A period of test and evaluation will be required, although it is expected that the remodelling of the software to replicate a RAFAT Hawk T.1 aircraft, that enables the Hawk Synthetic Training Facility at RAF Valley, will be ready for use in 2023. Collectively, this will aim, as far as possible, to accurately replicate flying scenarios for our pilots'.

It is difficult to convey just how trite, insincere and meaningless this is. It entirely omits, for example, that it is not only common sense but mandated that a simulator be *'truly representative'* of the aircraft flown. (I have explained where it *was* mandated, so if this has been changed then a deliberate decision has been made to deny correct training, and carry risks that are not recorded in the Risk Register). And the reply carefully avoids the question as to why it did not reflect the Red Arrows Build Standard and concept of use in the first place.

On the matter of the stall warner, Minister again misleads. He gives the impression that the modification was readily approved, when in fact it was initially rejected by Air Marshal Gray on 21 September 2021 as *'grossly disproportionate'*.

However, the response does mention Command Eject, when the Coroner did not. But it is presented as going above and beyond, a *'key enhancement'*, when it is no such thing. Once again, MoD simply does not grasp its own rules. Maintaining the build standard is not an enhancement. It is a mandated prerequisite to the fitness for purpose of the aircraft. And that is the elephant in the room.

12. The case for prosecuting MoD

Déjà vu

I have mentioned a number of previous fatal accidents. On each occasion it was families and members of the public who identified the anomalies in MoD's reports, uncovered and assessed what had been concealed, and revealed the truth. Of these cases, it could be said Hercules XV179 and Nimrod XV230 have been 'won'. While the Chinook ZD576 Board of Inquiry findings have been set aside and the deceased pilots cleared of gross negligence, it is often forgotten that the 29 families await a reopening of the Fatal Accident Inquiry, to hear the evidence concealed by MoD that forced the overturn. The others are also in abeyance because legal authorities will not act.

These accidents are only truly explicable by reference to the whole. The main systemic failing is that MoD could not demonstrate the aircraft types (not just the accident aircraft) were airworthy. In the Chinook and Nimrod cases this was accepted by the government. The Sea King ASaC Mk7 Board of Inquiry itself spelt it out. MoD admitted Tornado was not functionally safe. The Wiltshire Coroner agreed Hercules did not satisfy the regulations, MoD concealing evidence while accusing aircrew of lying over its existence. Also, that *'serious systemic failures'* in the RAF had robbed them of *'their opportunity for survival'*. Worst of all, in each case prior warning was given of root cause. But still MoD will not admit that the accidents are in any way connected.

Gross Negligence Manslaughter

The danger is always of individuals being blamed when Inquiries have identified factors outwith their control. Aircrew are told the aircraft is airworthy, serviceable and fit for purpose (three entirely different things), and must accept this. If they are not, then it is unsafe to accuse them. Here, MoD could not demonstrate any, so criticism of Flight Lieutenant Stark is improper.

But there is undeniable evidence that all elements of the offence apply to other known individuals, and across numerous fatal accidents. The only reason I would exclude most Ministers is lack of proximity. Nevertheless, many were given direct (verbal and written) notice, and refused to take action even after the warnings proved correct. The most notorious example is Minister of State Adam Ingram MP being advised of systemic airworthiness failings the *year before* the Nimrod XV230 accident; and denying them the year *after* when the cause was known.[84] His successor, Bob Ainsworth MP, continued in the same vein, five months *after* the Coroner had reiterated the failings.[85] Both were blatantly lied to by MoD staff. These actions were *truly exceptionally bad*.

The actions of those who signed the Hawk Releases to Service must be examined. I do not suggest theirs were the only infractions; but it is the logical starting point because they stated they were satisfied a valid Safety Case existed, and all risks to life were Tolerable and ALARP. But these mandated criteria had not been met. Moreover, the signatories were in a position of proximity, as all RAF personnel relied *directly* on their personal written assurance. These declarations exhibited a lack of diligence and *must* have been a conscious act, because the risks had occurred before and were the subject of previous recommendations to their department (the Air Staff).

While no signatory can know everything on all subjects, all staff have access to expert assistance. It is mandated in every aviation contract for just this purpose, and the procedures (if implemented) ensure this advice really is 'expert'. Thus, the persons who directed that these mandates must *not* be implemented are also answerable.

What must also be questioned is the culture that permits this. That means weeding out those who deny Duty Holders sufficient resources to meet their responsibilities, condone abrogation, and view safety as a cost to be avoided. It is difficult to see what place any military officer or civil servant can have in MoD when they eschew the integrity and competencies expected of them, and ignore legal obligations.

*

Here, the worst act, in terms of professional (in)competence and effect on the family, was the decision that passengers are expendable so long as the pilot survives. Who benefited? Clearly the RAF, and in particular 22 Group, because it can say the risk mitigation was successful, as Flight Lieutenant Stark survived. That Jon died is irrelevant. Harsh? It's there,

---

84 Letter 15 September 2005 to Adam Ingram MP, and reply D/Min(AF)/AI MC06559/2006, 17 May 2007. Nimrod XV230 crashed in the interim.

85 Letter D/Min(AF)/BA MC04733/2008, 14 October 2008, Bob Ainsworth MP to Steve Webb MP. The Inquest had been held in May 2008.

in black and white.

The Operating Duty Holder, Air Officer Commanding 22 Group, should have been in court to justify this. He was obliged, at regular intervals, to verify the risks were Tolerable and ALARP - so it doesn't matter that he wasn't there for the original decision. There were seven AOCs between 2006 and 2018; and they might also be able to explain the Air Cadet Glider fiasco. They didn't have a Safety Case either, were unairworthy, unserviceable and unfit for purpose. Knowing this, the RAF flew schoolchildren in them. *Truly...*

A full investigation would reveal a number of conflicts of interest; such as one AOC becoming Director General of the Military Aviation Authority, and then of the Defence Safety Authority. If he didn't understand the risks when he signed them off between July 2007 and April 2009, the penny must surely have dropped when instructed to implement the recommendations of the Nimrod Review, where the entire report concentrated on poor Safety and Risk Management.

In fact, so great are these issues, resulting in numerous avoidable deaths, and the removal from service of whole aircraft fleets, I suggest the Chief of the Defence Staff and the Secretary of State must answer. This is not just about 22 Group.

Corporate Manslaughter

To recap, the following needs to be proved by the prosecution:

1. The defendant is a qualifying organisation.

2. The organisation owed a relevant duty of care to the deceased.

3. There was a gross breach of that duty by the organisation.

4. The way in which its activities were managed or organised by its senior management was a substantial element in the breach.

5. The gross breach caused or contributed to the death.

I have explained why 'grossness' is the only issue in question, and why I believe MoD's conduct satisfies the *Misra* test of falling *'so far below the standard to be expected of a reasonably competent and careful person in the defendant's position that it was something truly exceptionally bad'*. The main evidence is the conscious nature of the breaches, repeated dissembling to families and courts, and non-disclosure of evidence. The degree is made worse by their relentless nature, over a period of decades.

141

I believe the best way to approach this is to ask:

1. *Is there a common root cause, the removal of which would have prevented all the accidents cited?* Yes. If mandated Standards had been implemented, the same root cause would have been removed from each accident sequence.

2. *Had senior MoD staff and responsible Ministers been advised?* Yes. And by accepting the Nimrod Review of 2009, the government admitted MoD had ignored the notifications. The breaches noted to the Coroner confirmed this as ongoing.

Senior staff condoned these actions, punishing those who insisted on implementing the regulations. In 2001 the issue was distilled down to one question: *What is the greater offence, the order to commit fraud, or the refusal?* Staff at 2- and 4-Star level ruled that only the refusal was an offence, and upheld disciplinary action for refusing to make false record in the airworthiness audit trail.[86] This ruling led directly to the nine deaths I mentioned in 2003 (Tornado ZG710, and Sea Kings XV650 & XV704). On 28 October 2014, Cabinet Secretary (the late) Sir Jeremy Heywood issued a written decision that it would be *'inappropriate'* to rescind the disciplinary action.

Recklessness and malice

Recklessness is more blameworthy than carelessness, but less culpable than malice. The next question is therefore: *Does this consciousness, and refusal to act in the face so many deaths, elevate the offence to recklessness, and was there a degree of malice?*

Historically, confusion has arisen from gross negligence manslaughter being sometimes known as reckless manslaughter, but this is no longer the case following *Adomako* and *Misra*. Although there is overlap, reckless manslaughter has a distinctly different meaning, and is held to be a state of mind where a person deliberately and unjustifiably pursues a course of action while consciously disregarding any risks arising from such action. The evidence shows this to be persistent practice in MoD.

I believe the conscious decisions to make *savings at the expense of safety*, and to ignore the direct warnings that proposed actions breached

---

86 For example, Loose Minute XD1(304), 10 January 2001, from Defence Procurement Agency Executive Director 1.

mandated regulations and increased risk to life, is overwhelming evidence of recklessness.[87]

There was no malice in this 1987 policy. The author, a Wing Commander, complained that his original intent was not understood by his superiors, who were then reluctant to admit their error and so carried on. Nor was there malice in the false declarations that aircraft were airworthy, although they were plainly deliberate and self-serving. (In other words, 'merely' reckless; but nevertheless illegal). But there was certainly malice in the decisions to discipline staff who pointed out the obvious risks to life, and the gross and deliberate waste of money, and who refused to make false record. Also, in the decision to blame staff (including deceased aircrew) who were known to be entirely innocent.

These ongoing failures, in the face of a mounting death toll and against a background of direct warnings, are so bad and so reprehensible as to amount to reckless negligence on the part of the decision-makers and those who condoned it.

The way ahead

I believe the way to restore deterrence and convey to future staff that the rule of law applies to them, is to lay a charge of corporate manslaughter against MoD. A clear message is required, one that will resonate throughout MoD. *Obligations are more than just words on paper, they must be met. Breaking the law will actually be punished.*

To this charge should be added MoD's repeated attempts to obstruct justice; documented, for example, by the Campbeltown Procurator Fiscal in 1996 after the Fatal Accident Inquiry into those killed in Chinook ZD576. A case infamous for the RAF's iniquitous, loathsome position that it was for the deceased pilots to clear themselves of the charge of gross negligence.[88] Once again, *truly exceptionally bad.*

I conclude that *all* the criteria for corporate manslaughter are met.

*

But there is more to this than 'simply' initiating a prosecution. The

---

87 Primary evidence set out in 'The Nimrod Review' (2009) and 'Submission to the Mull of Kintyre Review - A report discussing systemic airworthiness failings in MoD and how this affected the Chinook HC Mk2 in 1993/94'. (David Hill, 2011).

88 Mull of Kintyre Review, paragraph 6.2.9.

Crown Prosecution Service (CPS), police and Health and Safety Executive have also failed in their duty - by overlooking evidence and even admissions by MoD, and allowing it to judge its own case. This complicity, by those charged with upholding the law, is a considerable obstacle to both justice and the prevention of recurrence. Not least because of their tendency to view MoD not as a suspect, but as a co-prosecutor. I believe therefore that an argument can be made for handling such cases differently. One possibility is revisiting the suggestion of former Lord Advocate, Lord Ronald Murray, *'To establish a Justice Commissioner (Ombudsman) for Personnel of the Armed Forces'*. This was prompted by the official position on Chinook ZD576 (above), the aim being to provide someone independent to act on behalf of the deceased pilots and similarly wronged servicemen.

(There exists, of course, the Service Ombudsman, but he is limited and cannot, for example, accept a complaint from a third party, such as family member or friend; which is less than helpful to the bereaved).[89]

It would be helpful to co-opt, or appoint, an experienced accident investigator to provide technical advice. One possible solution is to have investigators, who in any case should be independent from the regulator and airworthiness authority, legally bound to the Coroner. (A suggestion often made by the Air Accidents Investigation Branch). This might also serve to temper the worst excesses of some Coroners.

Also, someone experienced in applying the 17 core components of maintaining a Build Standard. Their main task would be to create a Compliance Matrix; and, as stated earlier, one for the Release to Service. This is *precisely* the process used when constructing the evidence to the Nimrod and Mull of Kintyre Reviews. This would highlight systemic failings.

But the reluctance to prosecute Departments of State is deep-rooted, and there will be much political resistance. The CPS and police must do their duty and take cognisance of *all* the evidence, not just that which MoD condescends to disclose. That means knowing where to look and what to ask, and so again requires expert assistance. They must always bear in mind that MoD has repeatedly denied the existence of evidence, only for the public to submit it. No better example exists than the Air Staff's replies to Gayle regarding the loss of Hawk XX334 in 1992.

---

89 https://www.scoaf.org.uk/how-can-we-help-you/what-can-ombudsman-do

What of the Health and Safety Executive, its supposed investigation of Sean Cunningham's death exposed again as incompetent, and its prosecution of Martin-Baker corrupt? Why has it ignored the death of Jon Bayliss? The scale of its prosecutorial misconduct is breathtaking, and demands a full legal review. Ms Sutherland could start things rolling by informing the Attorney General of the facts. She would never know how many lives she would save, only that it would be many.

The political domain is where this can all be fixed, but is also where there will be most resistance. This was put well by former head of the Accidents Investigation Branch, the late William Tench, whom I have already mentioned:

'It is a matter of public record that when a certain accident occurred only one day after the political pendulum had swung over and a new administration had taken office, an irate MP demanded to know why the government had not taken steps to prevent such things taking place. That MP was the Minister of the previous administration having responsibility at the time for civil aviation. Such cynical behaviour and insincerity is a waste of parliamentary time and contributes nothing to improve the safety of flying, and neither does it affect the manner in which aircraft accident investigations are carried out'.

Few politicians, one notable exception being Lord (Norman) Tebbit, a former RAF pilot, have shown any interest in aviation safety. Of the current crop, Johnny Mercer MP, a former soldier and now Minister for Veterans' Affairs, takes a keen interest in another area - Northern Ireland veterans who are pursued with the government's support. But he faces time and resources constraints, and parliamentary ambivalence - especially from the Defence Select Committee, which he sits on. As a minimum, he should extend this concern to include the Chinook ZD576 widows, some of whom are still door-stepped by security forces seeking evidence (from diaries) to use against these soldiers (and former RUC officers). An Ombudsman would help his cause enormously.

*

On 29 April 2022, a formal complaint of corporate manslaughter against MoD was lodged with North Wales Police.[90] They did not reply.

---

90 E-mail 29 April 2022 17:56 to Chief Inspector Trystan Bevan, in reply to his e-mail 29 April 2022 13:10.

13. Conclusions

It is difficult to know where to draw the line and publish. Experience tells me the legal establishment will at best procrastinate, hoping the Bayliss family goes away. Often, one must be content that the facts have been made public and some good will come of me writing about it - the family has a degree of closure, and a good cause benefits.

Ironically, and to its credit, the Service Inquiry came closest to the truth:

'Whilst this was an air accident, the broader effects of resource constraints, pressures and tempo are equally applicable across Defence'.

These broader effects, and their cause, were already known to MoD. Like many before it, this case was characterised by a pre-determined plan to conceal long-term negligence and pernicious violations. The evidence given by MoD was a litany of lies. Yes, it admitted many breaches; but breathed a sigh of relief when greater breaches, in fact imprisonable offences, were not mentioned in court despite being notified in evidence. The official reaction, a report to the Secretary of State mentioning two issues unrelated to Jon's death, didn't even make the local news. Its cover-up has succeeded.

But now you are aware of the known facts, do you think these breaches gross? If so, then like me you will believe Jon's death manslaughter.

I cannot help but wonder if he would be still alive had the Health and Safety Executive taken action against MoD, instead of protecting it by prosecuting Martin-Baker in 2018. Or if MoD had implemented the 2009 Nimrod Review recommendations, or the Secretary of State's mandated regulations. Or if the Assistant Chief of the Air Staff and RAF Chief Engineer had heeded the 1992 warnings of the RAF Director of Flight Safety. Or the 1988 warnings from civilian staff as to the effects of RAF policy. So many missed opportunities.

This utter failure, this reckless negligence and disregard for life, deserves higher attention. Otherwise, MoD will continue on its killing spree.

David Hill, July 2022

Pen Portrait - Corporal Jonathan Bayliss

By Michael Bayliss and Gayle Todd (née Bayliss)

Much can be said about the life and career of our son and brother. He was a natural leader, dedicated and passionate about his role with the Royal Air Force. He was a kind, generous and compassionate son, brother, uncle, and friend. His death has left a huge void in the lives of so many colleagues, friends, and loved ones.

Jon was born on 13 February 1977 in Dartford, Kent. He went to Our Lady of Hartley Catholic Primary School and then to Longfield Middle with his elder sister Gayle. He attended Longfield Upper School in Kent before heading to West Kent College, where he graduated with an HND in engineering management from the University of Greenwich. Growing up, he loved the outdoors and was a Boy Scout, earning his Eagle Scout badge. At 11, he had his first experience with the RAF, joining the Air Training Corps.

After graduating, he started working at Brands Hatch racetrack, building rallycross cars. While there, an exciting opportunity arose to work for Foskers, a Ferrari specialist. Jon excelled, working on rare and valuable cars. On one occasion they sent him abroad to recover a classic Ferrari which had broken down. But as much as Jon loved his time there, he was looking for more. He joined the RAF in 2001, attending basic training at RAF Halton and another year of intensive training at RAF Cosford. His passing out parade saw a flyby of two Hawk Jets. His first posting was to 16 Squadron at RAF Coltishall. He acted as engineering support for the squadron's display aircraft. During his time there Jon was asked to lead a bike ride from base to St Omer, France raising money for the Royal Air Forces Association, looking after serving and retired service personnel.

He spent many tours of duty overseas, including the Falkland Islands, Cyprus, the Middle East, United States, China, and four months stationed in Afghanistan, which led to his promotion to Corporal. In 2015, Jon was offered the prestigious post of engineer with the Red Arrows at RAF Scampton. It was a posting he had dreamed about since a child. Two years later, he was named Number One Dye Team leader, and selected as a member of 'Circus' responsible for the servicing and maintenance of Red 3. Jon's career with the RAF began with a Hawk aircraft, and sadly ended in the same plane.

Jon received three medals during his RAF career - the Afghanistan campaign medal, long service and good conduct, and for his service during the Queen Elizabeth II Diamond Jubilee. His superiors held him in high regard noting:

'His excellent leadership and management qualities, effectiveness, judgment and powers of communication together with his positive attitude towards team spirit and service life in general fully justify his selection for promotion'.

'Professional in a multitude of situations, Bayliss has proven himself to be highly adaptable. When a suspect package was found in the passenger handling facility, understanding the potential severity of the situation, Bayliss offered his assistance to FP personnel. With true courage, he safely but swiftly cleared the parking ramps of personnel, and utilizing his polite but firm communication style and escorted off a reluctant 747 crew'.

'This totally competent, well-respected tradesman, is always first choice for the recovery of stranded aircraft all over the world. As part of a team tasked with recovering an aircraft with undercarriage problems from a foreign airbase, he was pivotal in the preparations to deploy. His knowledge allowed him to prepare the correct tools and paperwork whilst excellent communication skills allowed him to liaise with external agencies, ensuring that the specialist ground equipment was available and prepared'.

'Bayliss is an outstanding tradesman with an in-depth knowledge unrivalled by any of his peers on the squadron. I have no hesitation in endorsing the highest of promotion recommendations to this outstanding airman'.

'He is often found in the gym acting as a mentor, encouraging less natural sportsmen to increase their personal achievements. Bayliss devotes many of his free weekends assisting the national Forestry Commission with the organization, management and building of mountain bike trails- continuously raising the positive profile of the RAF'.

'A first-rate mentor to all, he can impart knowledge at the right level for anyone be they senior or junior'.

One winter, during the return from a detachment in China Lake, USA one of the jets developed a fault, the team diverting to a base on the Northeast Coast of the USA where the temperature was below zero. Jon worked for hours on the faulty Typhoon, exposed to the elements dressed in only desert fatigues. Such was his dedication that by the time the jet was repaired he was experiencing early stages of hypothermia. It took 3 months before he gained full sensation back in his fingers.

Posthumously, Air Chief Marshall Sir Stephen Hillier, spoke of his incredible career:

'Jon's natural leadership ability, outgoing personality and ability to communicate at every level meant that he was at the top of his game. Dealing with every situation with absolute commitment, the utmost professionalism and all with his infectious smile'.

RAF Scampton named the mess bar 'JB's' after their good friend, and RAF Valley created the 'Jon Bayliss Welfare Hub'. There are many memorials dedicated to him in both the UK and in America.

Jon was a gentle giant, a humble person, always willing to help others. He was a hard worker who always found a solution to the problem, often going beyond what was required, and he would never complain. His attention to detail was never more evident than when he jumped out the belly of a VC10 demanding a Tornado that was about to take off be halted. He sprinted over to the jet, airliners backing up behind them, closed an open panel on the aircraft, and then sprinted back to the VC10 to start the difficult task of re-boarding the huge aircraft via a net that had been thrown out the side door.

Jon was a loyal and discreet person who had many long-term friends both from childhood and service. He offered a roof over the heads of friends that had fallen on hard times in their marriages, and a shoulder to cry on for those struggling in their lives. He will always be remembered for his quick-witted dry sense of humour, always making people laugh and leaving many hanging awkwardly with his deadpan 'half-truths'. When asked his age, he would always reply with a straight face *'29'* and that was that, you'd never know his true age.

The loss of Jon in March 2018 continues to be felt by family and friends. His proud father fondly remembers how he always thought of others first, even as a young child. On one occasion he had a bag of sweets and offered them to all present, only to be left with nothing. He shrugged, smiled and said *'Oh well'*. He and his father enjoyed doing woodworking projects together and were always discussing their next projects. Jon was very close to his mother, Jennifer, whom he helped care for after she was diagnosed with dementia in 2017. He had intended that she would move in with him when it became too hard for her to live alone; sadly this was not to be and Jennifer's health deteriorated quickly after the accident and she passed away October 2020. His older sister Gayle cherishes the memories of their childhood and Jon's many visits to the United States to spend time with her and her family. He was the uncle and Godfather of Chloe and Ethan, whom he adored. He would regularly facetime and even partake in virtual tea parties and hide and seek. Shortly before his death, Jon and his partner of 4 years, Jemma, bought a home together and were making plans for their future life.

Now, nearly four years after his tragic death, Jon's family continues to honour him and his wishes. He left a note attached to his will that read; *'Oh well, shit happens, don't spend too much time crying about me. Get on with your lives because I had a really good one'.* While he knew there were risks involved with the career he loved so much, he never expected his life to be cut so short, at the young age of 41. His family wants others to learn from what happened and do whatever is necessary to protect his fellow servicemen and women.

Queen Elizabeth II once addressed the nation:

'There can be doubt, of course, that criticism is good for people and institutions that are part of public life. No institution... should expect to be free from the scrutiny of those who give it their loyalty and support, not to mention those who don't. This sort of questioning can also act, and it should do so, as an effective engine for change'.

Rest In Peace

Bibliography

1. 'The Hawk Story', Harry Fraser-Mitchell (2013).

2. Hawk T.1A XX204 Service Inquiry Report.

3. Defence Standard 05-125/2 - Procedures for Post Design Services.

4. Defence Standard 00-56 - Safety Management Requirements for Defence Systems.

5. Defence Standard 00-970 - Design and Airworthiness Requirements for Military Aircraft.

6. JSP 553 - Military Airworthiness Regulations.

7. Various Inspectorate of Flight Safety Airworthiness Review Team reports, including Chinook D/IFS(RAF)/125/30/2/1, 7 August 1992 and Nimrod D/IFS(RAF) 100/12/35, 24 July 1998.

8. D/IFS(RAF)/140/42/92/1 4/93 RAF Aircraft Accident Report Hawk T.1A XX334, 30 September 1992. Published 23 March 1993.

9. Red Arrows Display Directive, issued for each display season by Commandant Central Flying School, and approved by Air Officer Commanding 22 Group (now 1 Group).

10. FTP3225H - Hawk Training Manual. Previously AP3225H - Hawk Flying Training Tactics and Weapons (alternatively referred to as the Hawk T.1 Student Study Guide and Instructor Guide, and the Advanced Flying Training Student Study Guide).

11. 'Safety Is No Accident', William H. Tench (1985)

Terms and abbreviations

ADEN   Armament Development, Enfield.

ALARP   As Low As Reasonably Practicable

CFS   Central Flying School

CPS   Crown Prosecution Service

DA   Design Authority - an appointment bringing with it
            financial delegation from MoD; as distinct from Design
            Organisation, which is an approval.

DC   Design Custodian - a company undertaking Design
            Authority duties, but which does not own the Intellectual
            Property Rights.

DEC   Director(ates) of Equipment Capability

DDH   Delivery Duty Holder

DSA   Defence Safety Authority

FTP   Flying Training Publication

g   g-force, a measurement of the type of force per unit mass -
            typically acceleration - that causes a perception of weight.

HSE   Health and Safety Executive, part of the Department of
            Work and Pensions.

IAS   Indicated Airspeed

MAA   Military Aviation Authority

ODH   Operating Duty Holder

PEFATO   Practice Engine Failure After Take-Off

PDSO   Post Design Services Officer. A Design Authority
            employee, but appointed by MoD.

QC   Queen's Counsel

QFI   Qualified Flying Instructor

RA   Regulatory Article

RTS   Release to Service, the Master Airworthiness Reference.

SDH   Senior Duty Holder

Printed in Great Britain
by Amazon

84867847R00092